Is Medical Marijuana Necessary?

Bonnie Szumski and Jill Karson

INCONTROVERSY

ReferencePoint
Press®

San Diego, CA

About the Authors

Bonnie Szumski has been an editor and author of nonfiction books for 25 years. Jill Karson has been an editor and author of nonfiction books for young adults for 15 years.

© 2013 ReferencePoint Press, Inc.
Printed in the United States

For more information, contact:
ReferencePoint Press, Inc.
PO Box 27779
San Diego, CA 92198
www.ReferencePointPress.com

Picture Credits:
AP Images: 59, 67
© Randall Benton/ZUMA Press/Corbis: 7
© Bettmann/Corbis: 54
© Mark Constantini/San Francisco Chronicle/Corbis: 19
Steve Gschmeissner/Science Photo Library: 25
James King-Holmes/Science Photo Library: 14
Landov Media: 32
© Michael Macor/San Francisco Chronicle/Corbis: 77
Photo Researchers: 62
© Christian Schallert/Corbis: 72
Thinkstock/iStockphoto.com: 40
© Tim Wright/Corbis: 46

LIBRARY OF CONGRESS CATALOGING-IN-PUBLICATION DATA

Szumski, Bonnie, 1958-
  Is medical marijuana necessary? / by Bonnie Szumski and Jill Karson.
    p. cm. -- (Controversy series)
  Includes bibliographical references and index.
    ISBN 978-1-60152-458-4 (hardback) -- ISBN 1-60152-458-7 (hardback)
    1. Marijuana--Therapeutic use--United States. 2. Marijuana--Law and legislation--United States.
I. Karson, Jill. II. Title.
  RM666.C266S98   2013
  615.7'827--dc23
                                                                    2012011561

Contents

Foreword

In 2008, as the US economy and economies worldwide were falling into the worst recession since the Great Depression, most Americans had difficulty comprehending the complexity, magnitude, and scope of what was happening. As is often the case with a complex, controversial issue such as this historic global economic recession, looking at the problem as a whole can be overwhelming and often does not lead to understanding. One way to better comprehend such a large issue or event is to break it into smaller parts. The intricacies of global economic recession may be difficult to understand, but one can gain insight by instead beginning with an individual contributing factor, such as the real estate market. When examined through a narrower lens, complex issues become clearer and easier to evaluate.

This is the idea behind ReferencePoint Press's *In Controversy* series. The series examines the complex, controversial issues of the day by breaking them into smaller pieces. Rather than looking at the stem cell research debate as a whole, a title would examine an important aspect of the debate such as *Is Stem Cell Research Necessary?* or *Is Embryonic Stem Cell Research Ethical?* By studying the central issues of the debate individually, researchers gain a more solid and focused understanding of the topic as a whole.

Each book in the series provides a clear, insightful discussion of the issues, integrating facts and a variety of contrasting opinions for a solid, balanced perspective. Personal accounts and direct quotes from academic and professional experts, advocacy groups, politicians, and others enhance the narrative. Sidebars add depth to the discussion by expanding on important ideas and events. For quick reference, a list of key facts concludes every chapter. Source notes, an annotated organizations list, bibliography, and index provide student researchers with additional tools for papers and class discussion.

The *In Controversy* series also challenges students to think critically about issues, to improve their problem-solving skills, and to sharpen their ability to form educated opinions. As President Barack Obama stated in a March 2009 speech, success in the twenty-first century will not be measurable merely by students' ability to "fill in a bubble on a test but whether they possess 21st century skills like problem-solving and critical thinking and entrepreneurship and creativity." Those who possess these skills will have a strong foundation for whatever lies ahead.

No one can know for certain what sort of world awaits today's students. What we can assume, however, is that those who are inquisitive about a wide range of issues; open-minded to divergent views; aware of bias and opinion; and able to reason, reflect, and reconsider will be best prepared for the future. As the international development organization Oxfam notes, "Today's young people will grow up to be the citizens of the future: but what that future holds for them is uncertain. We can be quite confident, however, that they will be faced with decisions about a wide range of issues on which people have differing, contradictory views. If they are to develop as global citizens all young people should have the opportunity to engage with these controversial issues."

In Controversy helps today's students better prepare for tomorrow. An understanding of the complex issues that drive our world and the ability to think critically about them are essential components of contributing, competing, and succeeding in the twenty-first century.

A Human Story

In the debate over medical marijuana, the human side of the story is often lost. Since the passage of the first modern medical marijuana law in 1996 in California, thousands of patients who have used the drug have reported that it has helped to alleviate symptoms of their diseases. Accounts of people who have had severe pain from terminal cancer, nausea, uncontrollable muscle spasms, post-traumatic stress disorder (PTSD), Asperger's syndrome, HIV/AIDs, and many other medical problems claim they have experienced remarkable results with marijuana. One man recalls that his 74-year-old mother, who died of lung, liver, and breast cancer, could not keep any food down because of the chemotherapy treatments. He asked his father if he could give his mother marijuana. When his father agreed, he reports:

> Only seconds later [after being given marijuana], she began rubbing her stomach. I asked her how she felt. "I feel a little woozy but my stomach feels better!" She was eating minutes later and the woman was literally pulled out of the grave for two weeks before passing peacefully and without pain medication of any kind. . . . In spite of being ravaged by three different cancers, she didn't take a single prescription pain pill or a med of any kind, didn't need to. . . .
>
> After eating her first food in a while, she regained some strength and instead of needing help to get to the bathroom, got up under her own power and began walking. Her voice started sounding better, too. The change was nothing short of a miracle. With just a few breaths of MJ [marijuana] vapor every four or six hours she eliminated her nausea, increased her appetite, was able to keep the food she ate down, and restored her will to live.[1]

Supporters of medical marijuana in California protest a federal crackdown on dispensaries in 2011. The debate over medical marijuana pits concern about the harmful effects of drug use against concern for patients who seek relief from the pain and discomfort of illness.

This son not only saw the results in his mother, but also could not help comparing them with what might have happened if his mother had used conventional painkillers: "What drug can Glaxo [a pharmaceutical company] possibly create in a lab that effectively treats so many things at once, within seconds of taking, while being so gentle to the body?"[2]

Numerous personal stories cannot help but inspire empathy toward individuals who are helped by marijuana's effects. Yet these personal victories are countered by the fact that the use of medical

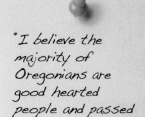

marijuana is still illegal in 34 states. Most states and the federal government believe that legalizing medical marijuana is simply too dangerous. Detractors claim that it leads to increased crime, recreational use, and addiction.

For many detractors, the needs of ill patients cannot override the harmful effects of legalization. The Oregon State Sheriff's Association, for example, believes that Oregon voters were naive when they passed the state's medical marijuana act in 1998. As one sheriff puts it: "I believe the majority of Oregonians are good hearted people and passed the initial Oregon Medical Marijuana laws with good intentions. They saw the ads of sick and dying patients and were willing to do anything to help an ailing person. However, the majority of patients for whom the program was intended is not who is using/abusing the Oregon Medical Marijuana Program."[3] The association and others believe that medical marijuana is being used primarily for recreational purposes by people who were never intended to have access to the drug.

Has empathy for the victims of diseases and disorders led to legalizing a drug that, overall, leads to dangerous changes in society? Numerous studies continue to be conducted in an attempt to answer this contentious question.

What Are the Origins of the Medical Marijuana Debate?

Medical marijuana has become an issue with many facets—human, political, and legal. While 16 states currently have made medical marijuana legal, these laws are in direct conflict with federal laws, which prohibit the use of marijuana. Along political lines, the issue becomes a rallying point for those who believe legalizing any drug inevitably leads to increased use and use among youth. Along human lines, those people who swear that marijuana has calmed nausea, dulled chronic pain, and relieved anxiety continue the fight for the right to use it therapeutically. Ironically, marijuana's history, in large part, stems from its medicinal use.

Even in ancient times, marijuana was used as a medicinal herb. Ancient texts show that *Cannabis sativa* was used in ancient Egypt, India, and Africa. New evidence continues to prove the herb's medicinal properties. In September 2008 two pounds of marijuana were found buried in a Chinese shaman's tomb that was over 2,700 years old. As Ethan Russo, the chief medical adviser for the Cannabinoid Research Institute writes about the discovery, "The cannabis was presumably employed by this culture as a medicinal or psychoactive agent, or an aid to divination. To our knowledge, these investigations provide the oldest documentation of cannabis as a pharmacologically active agent, and contribute to the medical and archaeological record of . . . this culture."[4]

The use and cultivation of marijuana has a long history in the United States as well. From the mid-1800s until 1937, marijuana was used for healing purposes by many physicians. In 1851 the *United States Dispensary*, a drug reference manual, recommended cannabis as a medical treatment for many afflictions:

> It has been found to cause sleep, to allay spasm, to compose nervous disquietude, and to relieve pain. In these respects it resembles opium; but it differs from the narcotic in not diminishing the appetite, checking the secretions, or constipating the bowels. . . . The complaints in which it has been specially recommended are neuralgia, gout, rheumatism, tetanus, hydrophobia, epidemic cholera, convulsions, chorea, hysteria, mental depression, delirium tremens, insanity and uterine hemorrhage.[5]

Cannabis was also included in the highly selective *United States Pharmacopoeia* (the authority for prescription and over-the-counter medicines) as a recognized medicine from 1854 until 1941. The early medical community in the United States, then, fully recognized marijuana's benefits in easing human ailments. Circumstances that allowed for marijuana to become an illegal, and often feared, substance did not arise until later in US history.

Marijuana's Demise

Marijuana's use became less recognized around the turn of the twentieth century. This was due, in part, to the fact that other effective pain relievers, such as morphine, began to be developed. Standardizing dosages was easier with these injectable drugs. A doctor could not reliably configure dosage for marijuana, which had to be smoked. In addition, different strains of marijuana had different potencies, and some took longer than others to take effect. This made it difficult to prescribe a regular amount. While its use as a medicine was becoming less important to physicians, however, marijuana was gaining a new user base—recreational drug users. Marijuana made regular appearances in hashish clubs that became popular in the United States during the late 1800s, for example.

Once marijuana became associated with recreational use, condemnation of the drug began to rise. Stories of marijuana's role in salacious and violent crimes, as well as information about its addictive properties, began to circulate. Because marijuana was usually brought into the United States from Mexico, border towns were particularly wary of the herb. El Paso, Texas, banned the use of marijuana (sometimes spelled *marihuana*) in 1914 because the city was a "hot bed of marihuana fiends," used primarily by "Negroes, prostitutes, pimps and a criminal class of whites,"[6] as one lawmaker put it.

One person particularly upset by marijuana's use was Harry Anslinger, who became the head of the Federal Bureau of Narcotics in 1930. Anslinger launched an antimarijuana campaign, using the mass media to spread his message. Often unsubstantiated, Anslinger's graphic and shocking accounts linked a variety of criminal cases to the drug. For example, Anslinger luridly describes in *American Magazine* the 1933 case of Victor Licata, who murdered his family while they were asleep:

> An entire family was murdered by a youthful addict in Florida. When officers arrived at the home, they found the youth staggering about in a human slaughterhouse. With an ax he had killed his father, mother, two brothers, and a sister. He seemed to be in a daze. . . . He had no recollection of having committed the multiple crimes. *The officers knew him ordinarily as a sane, rather quiet young man; now he was pitifully crazed.* They sought the reason. The boy said he had been in the habit of smoking something which youthful friends called "muggles," a childish name for marihuana.[7]

Other highly publicized accounts linked marijuana to other murders, suicides, and, in general, unrestrained criminal activity.

Managing a Life-Threatening Illness

George McMahon, the fifth legal recipient of marijuana from the federal government, describes how marijuana helped him manage a life-threatening illness:

> Since March of 1990 I have been receiving a monthly prescription for medical marijuana from the federal government for my medical problems. I am one of only 34 known medically ill individuals who have been approved to use marijuana legally in the U.S. I suffer from a rare neurological disease known as Nail Patella Syndrome (NPS). There are only 200 known cases of this genetic disorder. Of those, eight percent are affected with organ and immune system complications, which kills most of them by the age of 40.
>
> My sister died with NPS at age 44. My mother has NPS, but is only affected by slight joint deformities. When I was three, my father died at the age of 40 from a combination of tumors and tuberculosis. Today, in addition to fighting for my life, I am still wagering a battle with marijuana.
>
> Instead of legality for just a few others and myself I am fighting to help scores of medically ill individuals who haven't received the privilege to use the drug legally. If one ill individual can legally use the drug and get some relief from their pain, I feel I have succeeded with my mission.

George McMahon, "My Story," George McMahon's Home Page. www.trvnet.net.

Anslinger tried to have marijuana outlawed under the Harrison Act of 1914, which banned the unrestricted sale of morphine and opium, but he could find little support in the medical community for such a ban, even though he polled many physicians in his on-going campaign to ban the herb.

Yet another law would lead to marijuana's condemnation. Anslinger and the Federal Bureau of Narcotics had succeeded in using the media and highly publicized, yet dubious, criminal cases to increase public fear of the herb. In response, Congress enacted the Marihuana Tax Act of 1937. The act imposed a tax of one dollar an ounce on anyone using hemp, the fiber of the marijuana plant, for particular industrial or medical purposes. Growers who cultivated hemp and those who sold it were required to register with the government. Anyone caught using marijuana for any other unregistered purpose had to pay a tax of $100 an ounce. The act was mainly directed at recreational drug users, but it had a significant effect on physicians. Those who wished to continue recommending marijuana to their patients were required to complete a large and time-consuming amount of paperwork.

William Woodward, a medical doctor and lawyer for the American Medical Association, testified before Congress in 1937 that such a tax would preclude the use of marijuana for medical purposes: "Since the medicinal use of cannabis has not caused and is not causing addiction, the prevention of the use of the drug for medicinal purposes can accomplish no good end whatsoever. How far it may serve to deprive the public of the benefits of a drug that on further research may prove to be of substantial value, it is impossible to foresee."[8] Despite a lack of support by the medical community, by 1937 all 48 states (Hawaii and Alaska did not become states until the 1950s) had enacted laws against marijuana's use. Because of the tax and the registration rules, cannabis was removed from the *United States Pharmacopeia and National Formulary* in 1941.

> "Since the medicinal use of cannabis has not caused and is not causing addiction, the prevention of the use of the drug for medicinal purposes can accomplish no good end whatsoever."[8]
>
> — William Woodward, lawyer for the American Medical Association.

Controlled Substances Act

Attitudes about drug use changed considerably in the 1960s. By the end of the decade, the use of marijuana and other street drugs had increased considerably. To combat the heightened drug use and the perception that law enforcement was not adequately addressing the nation's burgeoning drug culture, Congress enacted the Comprehensive Drug Abuse Prevention and Control Act of 1970, which included the Controlled Substances Act (CSA). The CSA classifies psychoactive drugs in five schedules. Marijuana was classified as a Schedule 1 substance, the most restrictive class. This classification means that the drug has no medical use, has a high rate of addiction, and cannot be safely prescribed by a physician.

However, the public's attitude toward marijuana had been changing. One group in particular, the National Organization for the Reform of Marijuana Laws (NORML), was heavily involved in attempts to repeal marijuana's Schedule 1 classification. Only the courts, Congress, or the Drug Enforcement Administration

A worker bales hemp straw for use in paper and textiles. In the 1930s Congress imposed a tax on hemp grown for industrial and medical purposes.

(DEA) have the authority to change marijuana's schedule. In response to NORML's appeals, the administrator for the DEA further refined the criteria for a drug's being accepted as medically sound. The drug must have:

> (1) Scientifically determined and accepted knowledge of its chemistry; (2) scientific knowledge of its toxicology and pharmacology in animals; (3) effectiveness in human beings established through scientifically designed clinical trials; (4) general availability of this substance and information about its use; (5) recognition of its clinical use in generally accepted pharmacopeia, medical references, journals or textbooks; (6) specific indications for the treatment of recognized disorders; (7) recognition of its use by organizations or associations of physicians; and (8) recognition and use by a substantial segment of medical practitioners in the United States.[9]

Those who support the legalization of medical marijuana argue that such criteria are a catch-22—impossible because marijuana cannot gain widespread acceptance while it remains prohibited by its Schedule 1 classification.

Compassionate Use

Despite its classification as a Schedule I drug, many patients, physicians, lawmakers, and medical organizations argue that numerous studies support the use of marijuana for medical purposes. In the late 1970s some state governments began to pass laws to allow for the use of marijuana as medicine. New Mexico passed the first law allowing for the medical use of marijuana in 1978. In the late 1970s and 1980s, 33 states passed similar laws. These state laws proved difficult to execute. In order to bypass federal drug laws, states must establish research programs and get approval from the US Food and Drug Administration (FDA) to issue an Investigational New Drug (IND) application. While in this process, many states gave up on their new legislation. Yet 17 states persisted with their programs to use marijuana for the treatment of glaucoma and the nausea that accompanies chemotherapy. Yet all of these trial programs fell apart due to the many hurdles placed before the states to establish research programs. Eventually, 10 states, including New Mexico, managed to successfully establish programs.

Another way for patients to use medical marijuana was to petition the government for a personal IND. This, too, had many hurdles, including finding a physician willing to help the patient apply. In 1976 glaucoma sufferer Robert Randall was the first patient to receive a Compassionate IND for marijuana use. Randall

The Nation's Legal Marijuana Repository

Since 1968 the University of Mississippi has maintained a contract with the National Institute on Drug Abuse (NIDA) to grow marijuana for research purposes. It is the only legal operation of its kind in the United States. The marijuana is grown, harvested, and then shipped to licensed facilities across the country. To receive a supply, researchers must first obtain approval from the NIDA. In addition, the facility tests marijuana samples seized by police to determine potency and assess trends in the black market. It also investigates nonsmoking methods to ingest the medicinal compounds of marijuana.

All of these processes are closely monitored: The fields where the marijuana is grown are double fenced, with guards patrolling around the clock. The locked-down facilities where the marijuana is processed feature multiple alarm systems and motion detectors; camera systems are monitored remotely by the Drug Enforcement Administration. While the security efforts and regulatory requirements focus on limiting potential abuse of the drug, many medical marijuana advocates feel that the federal government has stymied research by making it difficult to obtain marijuana for research purposes.

won a case against the federal government using a legal precedent known as the "medical necessity defense." Randall was able to treat himself with government-grown marijuana. During the advent of the AIDS epidemic in the 1980s, many AIDs sufferers, unable to eat because of their severe nausea, also applied for Compassionate INDs. Very few were actually granted.

The lack of a Compassionate NID did not stop AIDS sufferers from turning to medical marijuana for relief. In the 1980s Dennis Peron was using marijuana to medicate his boyfriend, who was dying of AIDS, when police raided his home. He says: "Marijuana was [my boyfriend's] best medicine. The cops came in one night, while he was dying. . . . He was 90 pounds and was weak and frail and covered with Kaposi's Sarcoma lesions. He was the love of my life and I had to watch him from the top floor being beaten, with a gun to his head. And I decided they would never do this again."[10]

The Compassionate NID Program was extended in 1978 but was closed to new patients in 1991. James O. Mason, chief of the Public Health Service, announced that the program would be suspended largely because it contradicted then-president George H.W. Bush's antidrug programs. Mason said, "If it is perceived that the Public Health Service is going around giving marijuana to folks, there would be a perception that this stuff can't be so bad. . . . It gives a bad signal. I don't mind doing that if there is no other way of helping these people. . . . But there is not a shred of evidence that smoking marijuana assists a person with AIDs."[11]

> "If it is perceived that the Public Health Service is going around giving marijuana to folks, there would be a perception that this stuff can't be so bad. . . . It gives a bad signal."[11]
>
> — James O. Mason, former chief of the Public Health Service.

Establishing a Balanced Social Policy

Nevertheless, due to the anecdotal evidence of many marijuana users afflicted with nausea, glaucoma, or chronic pain, the government has found it difficult to completely shut out patients' and states' appeals to continue research into its efficacy. The US government has funded several studies that found restrictions on marijuana to be ineffective. For example, in its 1972 report, the National Commission on Marihuana and Drug Abuse concluded:

Society should seek to discourage use, while concentrating its attention on the prevention and treatment of heavy and very heavy use. The Commission feels that the criminalization of possession of marihuana for personal use is socially self-defeating as a means of achieving this objective. We have attempted to balance individual freedom on one hand and the obligation of the state to consider the wider social good on the other.

. . . Considering the range of social concerns in contemporary America, marihuana does not, in our considered judgment, rank very high. We would deemphasize marihuana as a problem. The existing social and legal policy is out of proportion to the individual and social harm engendered by the use of the drug. To replace it, we have attempted to design a suitable social policy, which we believe is fair, cautious and attuned to the social realities of our time.[12]

The report met fierce resistance. Despite the commission's recommendation to end marijuana prohibition, then-president Richard Nixon and Congress ignored the findings and refused to implement the recommended changes.

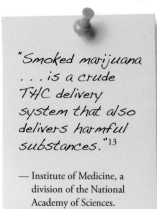

"Smoked marijuana . . . is a crude THC delivery system that also delivers harmful substances."[13]

— Institute of Medicine, a division of the National Academy of Sciences.

Gradually, even the government could not deny the efficacy of marijuana in treating some diseases. In 1999 the Institute of Medicine (IOM) issued a report. IOM is part of the National Academy of Sciences, a nongovernmental organization that conducts research on a variety of medical topics. Starting in 1997, IOM spent $1 million to conduct a comprehensive review of marijuana, holding three hearings to gather evidence for a report commissioned by the White House Office of National Drug Control Policy (ONDCP). The goal was to assess the potential health risks and benefits of marijuana. In the report, titled *Marijuana and Medicine: Assessing the Science Base*, the Institute of Medicine concluded: "Scientific data indicate the potential therapeutic value of cannabinoid drugs, primarily THC [the psychoactive chemical in marijuana], for pain relief, control of nausea and vomiting, and appetite stimulation;

smoked marijuana, however, is a crude THC delivery system that also delivers harmful substances."[13]

The report goes on to recommend the use of marijuana for certain patients: "Recommendation: Short-term use of smoked marijuana (less than six months) for patients with debilitating symptoms (such as intractable pain or vomiting)."[14] Yet the report qualifies that stance by frowning upon smoking as a marijuana delivery system. The report concludes that "until a nonsmoked rapid-onset cannabinoid drug delivery system becomes available, we acknowledge that there is no clear alternative for people suffering from chronic conditions that might be relieved by smoking marijuana, such as pain or AIDS wasting."[15]

Given that its own reports seemed to contradict the necessity of strict criminal laws governing marijuana, some government officials began to stand up for a relaxing of these restrictions.

A multiple sclerosis patient smokes marijuana to ease the pain and tremors caused by the disease. Early in the medical marijuana debate, the Institute of Medicine noted the benefits of short-term use of marijuana for certain types of pain but also remarked that alternatives to smoking the drug are needed.

Responding to the IOM report, former ONDCP director Barry McCaffrey stated in a 1999 letter to US secretary of health and human services Donna Shalala:

> This IOM study is the most comprehensive summary and analysis of what is known about the use of marijuana and its constituent cannabinoids for medicinal purposes, marijuana's mechanism of action, peer-reviewed literature on the uses of marijuana, and costs associated with various forms of the component chemical compounds in marijuana. We are hopeful that the discussion of the medical efficacy and safety of cannabinoids can now take place within the context of medicine and science.[16]

Like McCaffrey, many continue to question the need for criminal prosecution of those who use marijuana for medical purposes. In the years ahead members of both the House and Senate will continue to assess whether to continue federal prosecution of patients and providers or relax prohibitions.

Further Erosion of Marijuana Laws

While the government has been slow to decriminalize medical marijuana, states have moved forward in spite of such reluctance. States that have legalized medical marijuana are convinced by both the mounting medical evidence and the insistence by voters that such laws be passed. Since 1996, sixteen states—Alaska, Arizona, California, Colorado, Delaware, Hawaii, Maine, Michigan, Montana, Nevada, New Jersey, New Mexico, Oregon, Rhode Island, Washington, Vermont—and Washington, DC—have enacted medical marijuana laws that provide legal protection for seriously ill patients who use marijuana under a doctor's recommendation. Fifteen of these states use a system of ID cards to obtain prescriptions for marijuana. A patient must first obtain a doctor's recommendation then apply for an ID card through a state or county agency. Once a prescription is obtained, patients must obtain their marijuana from a state-controlled dis-

"We are hopeful that the discussion of the medical efficacy and safety of cannabinoids can now take place within the context of medicine and science."[16]

— Former ONDCP director Barry McCaffrey.

pensary. Yet, even with such state-run systems, medical marijuana users and dispensaries are still not safe from prosecution.

In California, federal prosecutors continue to raid and close dispensaries for not complying with federal law, even though these dispensaries are governed by state law. Although dispensaries are state-governed, some are less discriminating about where they obtain their marijuana. In the 2005 case of *Gonzales v. Raich*, the Supreme Court ruled that Congress could criminalize dispensing and use of marijuana even in states that have approved it for medical use. In that case, defendant Angel Raich used homegrown medical marijuana she obtained from grower Diane Monson. Using the marijuana was legal under California law, but illegal under federal law. The DEA raided and destroyed Monson's marijuana plants. Monson and Raich sued, arguing that DEA violated their constitutional rights. The Supreme Court ruled in favor of the DEA, saying that federal law supersedes state laws.

The result of that case has left open the legality of state-operated dispensaries ever since. Often federal government raids of dispensaries are due to issues of provenance—whether the marijuana was purchased from a state-approved grower. This is just one of the many conflicts that states have encountered when defending state law over federal law. Currently, lawyers who support dispensary owners bring the owner's case before a judge to prove that the owner was in compliance with California law. To date, California's dispensaries have successfully proved their cases and have been allowed to remain open.

A Continuing Issue

While the federal and state governments continue this battle, polls show that the American public overwhelmingly supports medical marijuana. A January 2010 ABC News/*Washington Post* poll found that 81 percent of Americans think "doctors should be allowed to prescribe marijuana for medical purposes to treat their patients."[17]

Yet while Americans may overwhelmingly agree on marijuana as medicine, many worry that its full legalization would lead to an increase in crime and in recreational use. Even when voters have passed legislation allowing medical marijuana, many people find dispensaries in their neighborhood objectionable and push for laws to govern where they can operate.

Clearly, medical marijuana continues to face many hurdles. As recently as May 2011, the US Department of Justice sent letters to a variety of state officials stating that they would prosecute states for cultivating and distributing medical marijuana. Similarly, in July 2011 the DEA ruled that marijuana "has no accepted medical use" and continues to deny attempts to reclassify marijuana to a less-restrictive drug classification. And yet for many patients, marijuana proves to be the most effective drug with the least side effects to treat their conditions.

Facts

- In China 5,000 years ago, marijuana was recommended as a treatment for malaria, constipation, and absentmindedness.

- Certain modern-day tribes in Africa use hemp to treat snake bite and alleviate the pain associated with childbirth.

- In the nineteenth century, cannabis was often administered as an alcohol-based extract that was swallowed.

- According to the Department of Health and Human Services, marijuana is the most commonly abused illicit drug in the United States.

- Many religious organizations, including the United Methodist Church, Presbyterian Church, Episcopal Church, and others, support the medical use of marijuana.

Is Marijuana Effective Medicine?

Determining whether any drug, including marijuana, is an effective medicine seems easy enough to prove. Clinical studies and patient trials begin the process and when completed, if successful, are submitted to the FDA, which governs and approves new medications. Yet, though marijuana's medicinal properties have been studied numerous times, it remains classified as an illegal substance in the United States. Not only is it illegal, its Schedule 1 classification marks it as highly dangerous and addictive. This classification, in large part, has complicated efforts to test marijuana's medical efficacy. Researchers have difficulty getting legal access to marijuana. Patients for clinical trials are also more difficult to find because of the stigma surrounding taking an illegal substance. Even when these hurdles are overcome, research studies are often small and limited in scope. The limited evidence poses formidable challenges for patients and doctors who want to use it as therapy.

Journalist Anna Wilde Mathews describes part of the problem: "The medical [landscape] remains confusing, largely because of limited scientific studies. A recent American Medical Association (AMA) review found fewer than 20 randomized, controlled clinical trials of smoked marijuana for

> "The medical [landscape] remains confusing, largely because of limited scientific studies."[18]
>
> — Journalist Anna Wilde Mathews.

all possible users. These involved around 300 people in all—well short of the evidence typically required for a pharmaceutical to be marketed in the U.S."[18]

The difficulty in obtaining permission to study marijuana for medical use in the United States remains daunting. For example, Lyle Craker is a researcher at the University of Massachusetts who has been trying to get a license from the DEA to cultivate marijuana for clinical research. He comments on the circular logic that inhibits research: "We can say that [marijuana] has no medical benefit because no tests have been done, and then we refuse to let you do any tests. The US has gotten into a bind, it has made cannabis out to be such a villain that people blindly say 'no.'"[19]

In spite of the difficulties presented in studying its use, researchers have completed and continue to complete studies into marijuana's use as a treatment. Among the areas of particular interest are its use in pain management, appetite enhancement, and seizure control.

The Endocannabinoid System

Although medical marijuana has been used for centuries, it had not been rigorously studied, largely because the medical community did not fully understand the human brain. It was not until the 1980s, when the endocannabinoid system was discovered, that scientists began to understand why marijuana may have therapeutic effects.

Cannabinoids are chemicals that occur naturally in the cannabis plant and in humans and other animals. These cannabinoids attach themselves to receptors in the brain, the organs, the immune system, and other areas. This endocannabinoid system is involved in regulating many body systems by turning certain functions off or on. Cannabinoids appear to help regulate appetite, movement, pain, memory, mood, immunity, inflammation, reproduction, and other bodily functions. Because marijuana also contains cannabinoids—more than 60 different kinds that may yield different properties—it can enhance the body's governance of these same functions. For example, cannabinoids such as THC, a component of marijuana, may stimulate receptors that create ap-

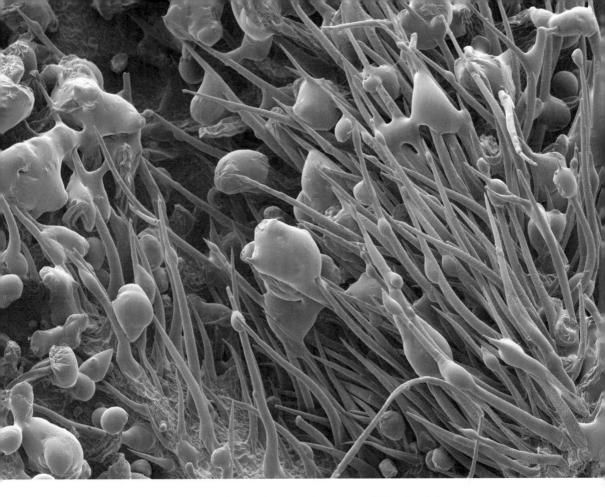

petite. THC and other cannabinoids may also turn off the body's pain receptors, slowing down or leading to fewer neural impulses, resulting in a decrease in the severity of pain. In fact, cannabinoids' therapeutic effects are well documented in three areas: their ability to inhibit pain, their ability to reduce nausea and spur appetite, and their ability to control muscle spasticity.

Pain Management

Some of the most promising research results involving medical marijuana focus on neuropathic pain, the most difficult kind of pain to treat. This type of pain often results in a burning hypersensitivity in the feet and legs and, less often, the hands and arms. Neuropathic pain affects millions of people and is difficult to treat with traditional pain medications. Neuropathic pain results when the nervous system is damaged, usually from a trauma such as a

Research shows that THC found in marijuana might have the ability to turn off pain receptors and stimulate receptors that create appetite. A colored scanning electron micrograph reveals THC crystals (brown) on the surface of marijuana (green).

stroke or infection or from a disease such as multiple sclerosis, diabetes, or AIDS. Some of the most groundbreaking research on pain has come out of the Center for Medicinal Cannabis Research (CMCR) at the University of California in San Diego. Since 2001, the center has produced four completed studies—the first clinical trials of smoked marijuana in the United States in 20 years—that indicate marijuana may indeed be useful in the treatment of pain.

Two studies focused on HIV patients. In 2007 a study on neuropathic pain related to HIV/AIDS was published in the *Journal of Neurology*. One of the complications of treating HIV/AIDS, as well as some other diseases, is that a patient is often nauseated and unable to keep from vomiting medications that must be swallowed. In this study, smoked marijuana effectively relieved a painful nerve disorder which affects roughly 30 percent of HIV/AIDS patients. Medications traditionally used for this type of pain do not work for all patients, may interfere with antiviral medications used to treat HIV/AIDS, and may have debilitating side effects that make them unacceptable for some patients. Daniel I. Abrams, professor of clinical medicine at the University of California at San Francisco, writes about the study's conclusion: "Smoked cannabis was well tolerated and effectively relieved chronic neuropathic pain from HIV-associated sensory neuropathy. The findings are comparable to oral drugs used for chronic neuropathic pain."[20] In a second CMCR study of HIV/AIDS patients published in 2008 in the journal *Neuropsychopharmacology*, one group smoked cannabis to relieve pain while a control group smoked placebo cigarettes. The group that used cannabis experienced significantly reduced pain over the control group.

Another CMCR study widened marijuana's use to patients whose neuropathic pain resulted from more diverse causes, including diabetes, spinal cord injury, and multiple sclerosis. The study, published in 2008 in the *Journal of Pain*, concluded that smoking cannabis significantly reduced neuropathic pain from diverse causes.

In another study completed in 2007 and published in the *Journal of Anesthesiology*, healthy volunteers were given skin injections of capsaicin (the fiery compound in chili peppers) to see if marijuana could ease the burning pain that resulted. Volunteers experienced significant pain relief after smoking marijuana.

All of these experiments proved that marijuana is successful in alleviating pain. However, subjects in the studies also reported the expected side effects of smoking the marijuana—feeling high and having diminished thought-processing capabilities such as reasoning and memory. Some research indicates that these side effects might be regulated by giving patients lower doses of the drug.

When Traditional Treatments Do Not Work

Commenting on the efficacy of cannabis in reducing pain, Igor Grant, director of the CMCR, says, "I was a little bit surprised, to tell the truth. . . . I somewhat expected that what we would get is a mixed result . . . which would not be so unusual. But the fact

Marijuana and Migraines

A migraine is a type of headache that is often associated with vomiting, nausea, sensitivity to light, throbbing pain, and other debilitating symptoms. Some medical organizations estimate that nearly 20 percent of Americans suffer from this type of headache. Many anecdotal reports have suggested that marijuana is an effective—and rapid—treatment for these patients. Some users even report that the onset of migraine can be prevented by marijuana if it is smoked when the first symptoms, such as ringing in the ears, appear. No clinical trials, however, have established that either smoked or oral forms of marijuana alleviate the symptoms of migraine. According to the National Migraine Association, most of the studies reported in medical literature are actually based on anecdotes as opposed to formal research. At the same time, several published studies suggest that marijuana can actually increase headaches.

that all of them came up with a consistent result makes me feel a little more comfortable in saying we could have something here."[21]

Grant also says the goal is not to replace more commonly prescribed pain medications but to use marijuana as an additional medication when others are unsuccessful: "Why do we need another antibiotic, another sleeping pill or antidepressant? The answer is, in part, because not everybody responds favorably to the drugs we have available. The reason isn't that pot is wonderful. It's that if it works, it's an alternative for some patients who aren't benefiting from traditional treatments."[22]

Other research has reached similar conclusions to those released by the CMCR. A trial at McGill University Health Centre published in a 2010 issue of the *Canadian Medical Association Journal* found that smoked marijuana offered modest pain reduction in patients suffering from neuropathic pain. Says Mark Ware, director of clinical research at the center and lead author of the study: "The patients we followed suffered from pain caused by injuries to the nervous system . . . which was not controlled using standard therapies. . . . This kind of pain occurs more frequently than many people recognize, and there are few effective treatments available. For these patients, medical cannabis is sometimes seen as their last hope."[23]

In addition to clinical studies, marijuana users themselves have supplied a preponderance of anecdotal evidence. As one woman says: "I am a 58-year-old conservative woman who has chronic sciatic pain. I was given opioids that I could not tolerate and then told I had to just bear it for all these years. And finally my son convinced me to try medical marijuana and I have to tell you that I had remarkable results with it. . . . I was just amazed by it."[24]

No Scientific Consensus

Other medical professionals remain unconvinced of marijuana's usefulness. Some think that marijuana's effectiveness is achieved merely through the feelings of psychological well-being it confers upon the user—the marijuana high—and that its medical use is extremely limited. Cecilia Hillard, a neuroscience professor at the Medical College of Wisconsin and past president of the International Cannabinoid Research Society, frames the debate: "It's hard to say how much people are really using it medicinally versus recreationally. . . . Right now we're sort of to a point where the claims of medical benefit are so numerous and over-the-top that you tend to get into the realm of, 'Well, I just don't believe any of this.' People are saying it's good for everything."[25]

Even though numerous studies have seemed to indicate marijuana's usefulness in pain relief, medical professionals have not reached a scientific consensus. Opponents contend that there is scant evidence that marijuana confers medical benefits not available with other well-established medicines already on the market. Randall J. Bjork, a neurologist practicing in Colorado Springs, Colorado, is just one skeptic of marijuana research. "There's research," he argues, "but its crappy research. It would be nice to see something definitive printed up in *The New England Journal of Medicine* or *Annals of Neurology*."[26] As yet, the FDA has refused to confer medical status upon marijuana, declaring that "no scientific studies support medical use of marijuana treatment in the United States."[27]

"Nausea, appetite loss, pain, and anxiety are all afflictions of wasting, and all can be mitigated by marijuana."[28]

— Institute of Medicine.

Treating Nausea and Bolstering Appetite

In addition to pain management, medical marijuana has a well-documented, beneficial effect for people suffering from nausea and loss of appetite. As the Institute of Medicine concluded after reviewing a body of scientific literature documenting marijuana's therapeutic value in 1999, "Nausea, appetite loss, pain, and anxiety are all afflictions of wasting, and all can be mitigated by marijuana."[28] Two groups particularly affected by these symptoms are cancer patients undergoing chemotherapy and patients with HIV infection.

Marijuana's effect on the appetite is well known by many people who have described what is anecdotally known as "the munchies," the desire to eat copious amounts of high-fat or sweet foods while high on the drug. The effect is a scientifically proven effect of THC, the main psychoactive ingredient in marijuana.

For people who experience nausea, such as cancer patients being treated with chemotherapy, eating is torture. Nausea and vomiting are common side effects. Nausea is so pronounced that taking traditional medications to treat it may also cause cancer patients to vomit. Marijuana, on the other hand, seems to stimulate the appetite and dull the impulse to vomit. A series of studies published from 2000 to 2009 were reviewed by the AMA, which concluded that marijuana improved appetite and calorie intake in cancer patients undergoing chemotherapy.

NIDA's Stance on Medical Marijuana

The National Institute on Drug Abuse is an agency of the National Institutes of Health that is charged with conducting research related to drug abuse and disseminating the results to inform public policy. The institute takes a strong stance against the recreational use of marijuana and concludes, moreover, that smoked marijuana makes an unlikely medication candidate:

> Marijuana is not an FDA approved medicine. . . . There are data supporting marijuana's potential therapeutic value for symptoms including pain relief, control of nausea, and appetite stimulation. However, there are several reasons why marijuana is an unlikely medication candidate: (1) it is an unpurified plant containing numerous chemicals with unknown health effects, (2) it is typically consumed by smoking further contributing to potential adverse effects, and its non-patentable status makes it an unattractive investment for pharmaceutical companies. The promise lies instead in medications developed from marijuana's active components, the cannabinoids, or (perhaps less so) for the development of alternative delivery systems for marijuana consumption.

National Institute on Drug Abuse, "Marijuana," May 2010. www.drugabuse.gov.

Scott Rozman, for example, was diagnosed with an aggressive form of cancer that required doctors to treat him with multiple rounds of chemotherapy directed at the middle of his chest. The intensity of the treatment caused Rozman to vomit 40 to 50 times a day. He lost 60 pounds in two months and was so weak the doctors feared he would not be able to complete the treatment. "The doctors thought I was a dead man,"[29] Rozman remembers. His doctors prescribed marijuana in the hope that he would be able to keep the nausea and vomiting at bay. The treatment worked; Rozman was able to eat, gain weight, and also become calmer and more relaxed during the grueling chemotherapy sessions. Many cancer patients report similar results from using the drug.

Similarly, patients suffering from HIV/AIDS also experience loss of appetite and extreme weight loss, called wasting. Studies of HIV/AIDS patients have shown that marijuana can trigger appetite and weight gain and help patients remain on life-extending treatment.

The medications used to treat hepatitis C, an infectious disease that affects the liver, can also cause debilitating nausea and vomiting. The effect is doubly aggravating because such patients must be on the medications for several months. The side effects make them stop taking the medication, increasing the chance of a relapse. Smoking marijuana appears to alleviate the nausea. A 2006 study published in the *European Journal of Gastroenterology & Hematology* reported that patients using marijuana as part of their therapy were more likely to complete their medication regimens, resulting in a 300 percent increase in successful treatment.

A Synthetic Alternative

So many cancer and HIV patients began using marijuana to lessen nausea and trigger appetite that the US government encouraged the approval of a synthetic form of the beneficial compounds in marijuana. In 1985 a synthetic form of delta-9-THC, one of the active forms of THC found in marijuana, was approved for medical use for these patients. Sold under the trade name Marinol, this synthetic drug was heralded as a way to solve the medical marijuana controversy. Those who found that marijuana alleviated their

A cancer patient smokes a marijuana cigarette. Studies have found that marijuana improves appetite and caloric intake in cancer patients who experience nausea and vomiting as a result of chemotherapy.

symptoms could now acquire a legal pill at a pharmacy and receive the same benefits as from an illegal substance. Marinol would also take away a common fear that made doctors reluctant to prescribe it—fear of addiction. As Herbert Kleber, professor of psychiatry at Columbia University and former deputy drug czar under President George H.W. Bush, says, "People don't abuse it."[30] Additionally, proponents of Marinol say that it has undergone rigorous research trials that have established its efficacy, safety, and dosing guidelines.

But Marinol has many detractors. The cost is one problem; Marinol can cost three to five times more than a dose of medical marijuana. In addition, some claim that it simply does not work. Ken Trainer, a 60-year-old who has battled multiple sclerosis for 25 years and smokes marijuana to calm the tremors in his arms and legs, says, "I felt no relief, I didn't feel ill, I felt nothing. It might as well be M&M's."[31]

Also, especially in the treatment of nausea, Marinol, because it is a pill just like other traditional medicines, may be difficult to swallow and may induce a round of vomiting. Dennis Peron, a longtime medical marijuana advocate, said: "Our patients at the Buyer's Club [a medical marijuana dispensary] who have tried it say it made them so stoned they couldn't function or that it had other adverse effects. Also, Marinol is a pill, so you have to keep it down long enough to help the nausea. That's nuts and it doesn't work."[32]

Taking a pill is another issue for many patients because it must be digested, and its effects are slower than a marijuana cigarette. As one user says: "Several years ago, I contracted a case of food poisoning. The frequent vomiting and diarrhea were unpleasant, but the feeling of nausea was the worst effect of all. In response, I smoked a few puffs of high-quality marijuana. The effects of the nausea disappeared after about 30 seconds. . . . Marijuana is the fastest-acting and most effective anti-nausea agent available."[33]

Muscle Control

The endocannabinoid system also controls movement. Because of its effect on this system, marijuana can help alleviate the symptoms associated with diseases that affect muscular control. These symptoms include seizures and spastic movements of the arms and legs that are commonly seen with illnesses such as multiple sclerosis and epilepsy.

Multiple sclerosis (MS), for example, is a neurodegenerative disease that results in an array of symptoms, including muscle rigidity, tingling and prickling of the hands and feet, painful muscle cramps, tremors, chronic pain in the extremities, and bladder problems. Some multiple sclerosis patients claim marked improvement of their symptoms with the use of marijuana. In a study completed at the CMCR, a placebo-controlled, randomized clinical trial was performed on 30 multiple sclerosis patients to test whether spasticity and muscle functionality was improved with the use of marijuana. Initial results of the study, presented in 2007 at the American College of Neuropsychopharmacology meeting, found that cannabis could "significantly reduce both an objective measure of spasticity, and pain intensity . . . and [it] provided some benefit beyond currently prescribed treatments."[34]

The CMCR is not the only research institute performing studies on marijuana's effect on uncontrolled movement. Thirteen controlled studies have looked at whether marijuana is a useful treatment for unwanted muscle movement. Results are mixed. One of the first reports from 1982 found "substantial evidence from animal studies to indicate that cannabinoids are effective at blocking seizures."[35]

A 2004 study in the journal *Neurology* reached far different conclusions, however. Lead researcher Patrick Fox writes about marijuana's effect on tremors associated with MS: "Analysis of the data showed no significant improvement in any of the objective measures of upper limb tremor with cannabis extract compared to placebo. . . . Cannabis extract does not produce a functionally significant improvement in MS-associated tremor."[36] In contrast, a more recent study, published in 2011 in the *European Journal of Neurology*, found that Sativex (a cannabis-based prescription mouth spray used to treat spasticity) improved spasticity in patients with MS who had not responded to other antispasmodic medications.

Still, these trials are clinically small, and the jury is still out on whether marijuana can significantly reduce unwanted muscle movement. Numerous anecdotal reports, however, suggest that marijuana can largely ameliorate these symptoms. As Trainer explains, "If I smoke a joint, the tremors go away most times before the joint is gone. . . . It makes my life a little easier."[37] Trainer claims, moreover, that Marinol did not have the same effect.

People afflicted with the uncontrollable seizures typical of epilepsy have also experienced relief through the use of marijuana. A 27-year-old epilepsy patient who uses it to control epileptic seizures reports: "I used to be on approximately 14 different prescriptions, and I would still have up to 12 seizures a day. I used to have to take two handfuls of pills. No more."[38]

Critics like Eric Voth of the Institute on Global Drug Policy are skeptical of such claims: "I'm very suspicious about it because for someone to have been on 14 medications and not solve her

"If I smoke a joint, the tremors go away most times before the joint is gone. . . . It makes my life a little easier."[37]

— Ken Trainer, who uses marijuana to alleviate symptoms of multiple sclerosis.

problems, and then have this miraculous benefit from one medicine, I just find that suspect."[39]

Other Disorders

Because of its effect on relaxing nerves, marijuana has shown some effectiveness in treating glaucoma, a serious eye disorder marked by an increase in intraocular pressure. If left untreated, glaucoma can lead to blindness. In fact, glaucoma is the leading cause of blindness in the United States. Many advocates believe that marijuana can reduce this pressure and slow or even stop the progression of the disorder. While many anecdotal reports exist, only a smattering of studies has researched marijuana as a treatment for the disorder. Consequently, experts have differing views on the subject of marijuana as a treatment for glaucoma. The Mayo Clinic, a world-renowned medical practice and research group, has indicated it is open to the possibility that some forms of THC might benefit glaucoma patients. In a 2011 article the Mayo Clinic stated that more research is needed but that some evidence suggests that THC, when taken under the tongue, may reduce eye pressure. Based on studies that began in the 1970s, the National Eye Institute has a different view:

> None of these studies demonstrated that marijuana—or any of its components—could lower IOP [intraocular pressure] as effectively as drugs already on the market. In addition, some potentially serious side effects were noted, including an increased heart rate and a decrease in blood pressure in studies using smoked marijuana.[40]

In addition, pioneering research is being conducted on people suffering from certain neuromuscular traumas and diseases, including spinal cord injuries, Parkinson's disease, and Huntington's disease. For now, these studies are too new to draw any definitive conclusions.

At the same time, a host of other disorders remain under investigation as to marijuana's usefulness in their treatment. Some evidence suggests cannabis can alleviate symptoms of immune disorders such as rheumatoid arthritis, fibromyalgia, migraines, menstrual cramps, and even irritable bowel syndrome. Again, most of this evidence remains anecdotal.

Future Trends

Whereas much of the research to date has measured marijuana's ability to alleviate symptoms of disease, much of the future research will focus on its potential to treat the disease itself. For example, marijuana may be used to moderate autoimmune disorders or neurological disorders such as Alzheimer's. Cannabis has also been shown to inhibit the growth of malignant tumors in animals. Studies on mice and rats have shown that cannabinoids may inhibit tumor growth, cause cell death, block cell growth, and block the development of blood vessels that tumors need to grow.

In some bastions of the medical community, especially those that deal with chronic pain, marijuana is increasingly being accepted and recommended. The American Medical Association (AMA) has adopted a somewhat favorable position that "calls for further adequate and well-controlled studies of marijuana," also stating that "effective patient care requires the free and unfettered exchange of information on treatment alternatives and that discussion of these alternatives between physicians and patients should not subject either party to criminal sanctions."[41]

Yet as far as the federal government is concerned, marijuana remains an unproven medicine and a prohibited substance. Many federal agencies, such as the FDA, continue to view marijuana as having "no currently accepted medical use."[42]

Government agencies are especially fearful that legalizing medical marijuana will simply lead to legalization of a substance that is addictive and potentially dangerous. For example, San Diego County district attorney Bonnie M. Dumanis decries the uptick in medical marijuana dispensaries in her area. "These so-called 'marijuana dispensaries' are nothing more than for-profit storefront drug dealing operations run by drug dealers hiding behind the state's medical marijuana laws."[43]

"These so-called 'marijuana dispensaries' are nothing more than for-profit storefront drug dealing operations run by drug dealers hiding behind the state's medical marijuana laws."[43]

— San Diego County district attorney Bonnie M. Dumanis.

Doubts about whether legal medical marijuana and illegal recreational use can coexist may be one of the main reasons legislators are cautious about the use of medical marijuana. For the United States, the conclusions are likely to be decided in the courts at some point in the future.

Facts

- A 2006 study published in the American Journal of Surgery found that oral THC significantly reduced the postoperative nausea and vomiting in breast cancer surgery patients.

- According to an assessment at the University of North Carolina at Chapel Hill, there is no conclusive evidence that marijuana effectively reduces pain.

- A study at the University of Iowa found that 5 to 10 mg of orally administered THC was as effective as 60 mg of codeine for treating pain associated with terminal cancer.

- A poll by ABC News and the *Washington Post* in January 2010 found that 81 percent of Americans support the right of doctors to prescribe marijuana for medical purposes.

- A 2009 study found that long-term marijuana smoking—over a period of approximately 20 years—was associated with a reduced risk of head and neck cancer.

CHAPTER THREE

What Are the Risks of Medical Marijuana?

Since the 1950s, when more Americans began using marijuana for recreational purposes, the drug has been both vilified and praised. Studies have actually contributed to mixed public sentiments on marijuana's medicinal value. Some reports have found that marijuana is effective at alleviating pain and enhancing appetite. Others suggest that the use of marijuana carries risks, such as potential addiction. Whether these risks outweigh marijuana's potential medical benefits continues to be studied.

Addiction

One of the most persistent concerns over marijuana's risks is whether it is an addictive substance. Many marijuana advocates state that, unlike many other medical treatments, marijuana carries no risk of serious addiction or side effects. These proponents argue that this gives marijuana a huge advantage when weighing whether medical use should be legally sanctioned. Researchers studying whether marijuana is addictive use a common definition. A drug is considered addictive if a person exhibits tolerance, in other words, must take more of the drug to get the same effects, and if ceasing the drug's use causes a person to go through physical and emotional withdrawal symptoms. Researchers have not been able to provide evidence that marijuana users exhibit any of these symptoms.

Many supporters conclude that compared with alcohol, heroin, nicotine, and even caffeine, the dependency potential of marijuana is relatively low. In the 1990s, researchers from the University of California at San Francisco and NIDA independently compared cannabis with alcohol, nicotine, cocaine, and heroin. Both sets of researchers concluded that cannabis carried the lowest overall risk of dependency of all of these substances.

Despite these conclusions, anecdotal evidence seems to suggest that chronic users do experience symptoms of dependence. According to the US Substance Abuse and Mental Health Services Administration, marijuana is the most often cited illicit drug for people seeking treatment. R. Gil Kerlikowske, director of ONDCP, states, "Several studies have shown that marijuana dependence is real and causes harm. . . . The lifetime prevalence of marijuana dependence in the US population is higher than that for any other illicit drug. Those dependent on marijuana often show signs of withdrawal and compulsive behavior."[44]

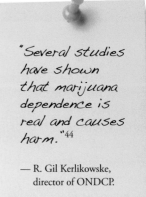

"Several studies have shown that marijuana dependence is real and causes harm."[44]

— R. Gil Kerlikowske, director of ONDCP.

Many users describe themselves as using marijuana compulsively and excessively. Joyce, a 52-year-old writer in Manhattan, describes how she started smoking pot when she was 15, after which it became an obsession: "I would come home from work, close my door, have my bong, my food, my music and my dog, and I wouldn't see another person until I went to work the next day. . . . What kind of life is that? I did that for 20 years."[45]

Herbert Kleber commented in 2009, "Marijuana addiction is becoming common and as a result I'm seeing an increasing number of people who have trouble stopping [their use of] marijuana. . . . Contrary to popular beliefs that there is no marijuana withdrawal, there is marijuana withdrawal. It's very clear cut."[46]

More Powerful Marijuana

One complication with older studies is the fact that recent strains of marijuana are far more powerful and yield far higher concentrations of THC. Some addiction experts wonder whether this factor might change marijuana's addictive properties. As Nora Volkow, director of NIDA, describes the problem, "It's like drinking beer versus drinking whiskey. . . . If you only have access to whiskey,

Most people who use medical marijuana smoke it in the form of a hand-rolled cigarette (pictured). Some research suggests that smoking marijuana might be just as harmful as smoking cigarettes.

your risk is going to be greater for addiction. Now that people have access to very high potency marijuana, the game is different."[47]

Proponents contend that more powerful marijuana would be highly unlikely to lead to a compulsion to use more because marijuana is not physically addicting compared with other drugs, such as alcohol or opiates. Even if a very large dose is consumed, confusion, agitation, and sedation generally result. These symptoms usually last only three to four hours, however—the time it generally takes for marijuana to be fully metabolized and excreted from the body.

The debate is not likely to end anytime soon. As Igor Grant states, there are

> two directions of misconception. The one side is people who believe that this is a very harmful drug, it's addicting, that it will damage your brain, it will damage your lungs, cause cancer, all sorts of things like this, that it's a gateway drug and so forth. I think that these concerns are quite overstated. . . . On the other side, though, are people who say it's a perfectly harmless drug, and that's not true either. It does have dependence producing properties. People sometimes have real trouble stopping using marijuana. It can affect their day-to-day life. So that's not good either.[48]

At least in clinical studies, marijuana has not proved to be physically addicting in the same way as opiates and other drugs are. Yet anecdotal evidence suggests that marijuana may engage some users in a psychological dependence. The final answers require further study. While addiction may be less of a concern, other risks continue to be studied.

Medical Concerns

The primary delivery system for marijuana is a hand-rolled cigarette that is smoked. With international attention focused on the effects of tobacco smoke on human health, specifically as a cause of cancer, researchers have feared the same outcomes for marijuana users. When a conventional cigarette is burned, toxic compounds, including carbon monoxide, tar, cancer-causing chemicals, and other by-products are created. Through the years, many government officials have stated that marijuana smoke is just as harmful, if not more so, than cigarette smoke. A November 2002 study by the British Lung Foundation concluded that marijuana contains many of the same chemicals as tobacco cigarettes and that it weakens the lungs and, consequently, the immune system, in the same way. The study concludes that "cannabis smoking is likely to weaken the immune system. Infections of the lung are due to a combination of smoking-related damage to the cells lining the bronchial passages and impairment of the principal immune cells in the small air sacs caused by cannabis."[49] The foundation claims that three to four marijuana cigarettes a day are as dangerous to the lungs as 20 or more tobacco cigarettes a day.

In fact, some researchers speculate that the only reason more marijuana users do not suffer serious effects from smoking is that marijuana is used differently than tobacco. A tobacco smoker might smoke a pack (20) a day, while a marijuana user is more likely to smoke one to three marijuana cigarettes a day.

More recent studies have failed to corroborate that marijuana is as harmful to the lungs and immune system as tobacco smoking. A UCLA study presented on May 24, 2006, by Donald Tashkin, a leading expert on the respiratory effects of illicit drugs, found no association between marijuana and lung cancer, even among heavy marijuana smokers. Tashkin states, "We hypothesized that there would be a positive association between marijuana use and

Negative Psychological Effects

Many users report that marijuana, whether used recreationally or medically, confers an abundance of negative psychological effects. As one user reports:

> Smoking pot heavily makes me super lazy. I struggle to get the most basic tasks, like housework, done on time. I was always a procrastinator, but smoking pot and being a procrastinator is a horrible combination. . . . I become easily distracted and struggle to get tasks finished. I used to be able to work for hours without noticing the time go by. . . . Sometimes I fade out when people are talking to me and I begin to daydream, or just shut down altogether. . . . I forget things. Wallet, keys, clothing, important dates, birth dates, names of people I was just introduced to, or the fact that I was just introduced to them. Smoking marijuana seems to affect my ability to transfer thoughts or ideas from short term to long term memory.

Marijuana Addiction Help, "Why I Quit Smoking Pot," blog. www.marijuana-addict.com.

lung cancer, and that the association would be more positive with heavier use. What we found instead was no association at all, and even a suggestion of some protective effect."[50]

As with other studies of marijuana, some of its chemical compounds seem to be both cause and cure. A 2005 study led by Robert Melamede, chair of the Biology Department at the University of Colorado, found that far from causing lung cancer, marijuana may actually kill cancer cells while sparing healthy cells. As Melamede says, "While both tobacco and cannabis smoke have similar properties chemically, their pharmacological activities differ greatly. Components of cannabis smoke minimize some carcinogenic pathways whereas tobacco smoke enhances some."[51]

Yet the largest, longest, and most recent study to date has found little relationship between lung cancer and marijuana smoking. A 20-year study published in January 2012 in the *Journal of the American Medical Association* concluded that marijuana does not impair lung function. As lead author of the study Mark Pletcher writes: "Marijuana may have beneficial effects on pain control, appetite, mood, and management of other chronic symptoms. Our findings suggest that occasional use of marijuana for these or other purposes may not be associated with adverse consequences on pulmonary function." Despite these positive findings, Pletcher notes that "it is more difficult to estimate the potential effects of regular heavy use, because this pattern of use is relatively rare in our study sample."[52]

Multiple Delivery Modes

Today, the point may even be less important. Marijuana users have found other ways to use the drug. Some use a special vaporizer to inhale the drug. During vaporization, marijuana is heated and the medically active cannabinoids are released in vapor form, without smoke and its harmful by-products. A study by Donald I. Abrams in 2007 found that inhaling vapors is an effective mode of delivery, producing blood levels of THC similar to those produced when marijuana is smoked but with no adverse effect on the lungs.

Other methods of delivery could mitigate concerns about lung damage. Marinol, which delivers THC in a legally prescribed pill, or eating marijuana in a baked good or candy, or boiling it and reducing it in a tincture, are all methods for ingesting the drug that do not require burning. Yet these methods take longer to produce effects because all of them require that the drug be digested and absorbed into the bloodstream. Many proponents believe that inhaling smoked marijuana is the quickest, most effective mode of delivery because the drug's effects are felt almost instantly.

Motor Skills and Cognitive Function

Many people oppose the legalization of medical marijuana because they fear it will become like other legal drugs, such as alcohol, a societal problem. Marijuana affects motor skills, and its use could impair driving, for example. A large body of research has explored whether marijuana plays a significant role in traffic accidents. Results are mixed. A 2004 report by the National Highway Traffic Safety Administration concludes that "marijuana has been shown to impair performance on driving simulator tasks and on open and closed driving courses for up to approximately 3 hours."[53] This can result in decreased car handling performance and increased reaction times. Other studies indicate that the impairment is mild, however, and does not play a significant role in traffic accidents. A 2011 study by IZA, a nonprofit research organization, even reports that fatal car crashes decreased by 9 percent in states that legalized medical marijuana, possibly because people may be substituting marijuana for alcohol.

Marijuana may also impair cognitive function, and its use could negatively impact learning. Kerlikowske declared in a 2010 speech that "prolonged [marijuana] use is associated with lower test scores and lower educational attainment because during periods of intoxication the drug affects the ability to learn and process information, thus influencing attention, concentration, and short-term memory."[54]

Researchers continue to study marijuana's effect on cognitive function. New research seems to indicate that marijuana causes a reduction in the ability to concentrate as well as in other cognitive functioning, such as memory. Many opponents of medical marijuana cite a historic study reported in *Biological Psychiatry* in 1980. Conducted by Robert G. Heath, then-chairman of the Department of Psychology and Neurology at Tulane University, the study claimed that marijuana killed brain cells in monkeys that had been given large doses. Proponents claim that these studies have been discredited by a series of animal studies conducted in the early 1990s. These studies by the National Center for Toxicological Research and SRI International found no evidence of physical changes in the brains of rhesus monkeys who received daily doses of marijuana for up to a year. Human studies found that heavy marijuana

"During periods of [marijuana] intoxication the drug affects the ability to learn and process information, thus influencing attention, concentration, and short-term memory."[54]

— R. Gil Kerlikowske, director of ONDCP.

users in Jamaica and Costa Rica showed no evidence of abnormalities in their brains.

Yet proof that other cognitive function is affected seems to be gaining. Heavy marijuana use can cause short-term memory deficits, diminish concentration, and impair learning. A 2011 study reported in the journal *Neurology* found that marijuana use by patients with multiple sclerosis (MS) resulted in cognitive deterioration. Anthony Feinstein, professor of psychiatry at the University of Toronto, reports the results: "Cannabis users performed significantly more poorly than nonusers on measures of information processing speed, working memory, executive functions, and visuospatial perception [visual and spatial awareness]."[55]

Reversible Effects?

The effects could be more pronounced for marijuana users who begin early in life. Staci Gruber, assistant professor of psychiatry at Harvard Medical School, performed a small but statistically significant study of marijuana users who began smoking it at the age of 16. No participant was older than 22. The study showed that the cognitive function of these users was significantly worse than both nonsmokers and those who had started using later in life. Gruber noted that "the findings were more striking than I had anticipated."[56]

Other medical professionals, including Donna Seger, professor of clinical medicine at Vanderbilt University, found Gruber's study unsurprising: "These results are true for most drugs. If you start doing any drug at an early age, you're working with an immature nervous system that is vulnerable to the effects of those drugs."[57]

Many proponents of medical marijuana charge that these types of effects subside—usually completely—as the drug wears off. Although some residual impairment has been noted in chronic marijuana users up to 12 weeks after quitting, a 2011 study at the Centre for Mental Health Research at Australian National University found no lingering, permanent effect on cognition. Robert Tait, author of the study concludes, "The adverse impacts of

"The adverse impacts of cannabis use on cognitive functions either appear to be related to pre-existing factors or are reversible . . . even after potentially extended periods of use."[58]

— Robert Tait, researcher at the Centre for Mental Health Research at Australian National University.

45

Critics of legalizing medical marijuana worry that the drug's effect on motor skills and reaction time will add yet another hazard on the road and ultimately lead to more traffic accidents.

cannabis use on cognitive functions either appear to be related to pre-existing factors or are reversible . . . even after potentially extended periods of use."[58] Many claim, moreover, that the temporary effects of marijuana intoxication are to be expected with any mind-altering substance—such as morphine, alcohol, and many other legal substances—and should therefore not negate marijuana as effective medicine.

Depression and Other Mood Disorders

While many believe that marijuana's ability to elevate mood can help people cope with depression, a small number of users have reported that marijuana actually causes depression and other troubling side effects. While the link between marijuana and depression has not been definitive either way, several studies have found a correlation between the two. For example, a 2009 German study found that "chronic cannabis use has been found to be associated with major depression."[59] Some evidence suggests that the depressive effects of the drug may be delayed, especially among young women who become depressed only later in life.

Another commonly reported side effect is acute anxiety and panic. Although no studies have definitively linked marijuana to anxiety disorders, anecdotal reports continue to accumulate. As one user describes his reaction to marijuana, "I first experienced panic when I was 17 after having marijuana. It was so extreme the word *panic* doesn't seem strong enough. It was more like absolute *terror*."[60] People who are seriously ill could have their symptoms magnified by such a fear response.

This type of discussion is an issue that surrounds many other reported side effects of marijuana. Does marijuana cause depression or other disorders, or do such disorders cause sufferers to seek out marijuana to alleviate these symptoms? Oscar Bukstein, associate professor of psychiatry at the University of Pittsburgh School of Medicine, explains that marijuana use, depression, and other forms of mental disorders often go hand in hand: "Many kids get high not to stay low."[61]

Schizophrenia

The link between marijuana and other mental disorders is especially troubling. For example, marijuana use has been linked to the onset of schizophrenia and other forms of psychosis. Several studies have suggested that exposure to cannabis during adolescence increases the risk of psychosis later in life.

One significant 2011 study at the University of Amsterdam found an association between marijuana use and the onset of psychosis. D.H. Linszen, professor of psychiatry and lead researcher, concludes, "Our results provide support that cannabis use plays an important role in the development of psychosis in vulnerable individuals. Cannabis use in early adolescence should be discouraged."[62]

Other studies seem to confirm such conclusions. Joseph M. Pierre, chief physician at the Schizophrenia Treatment Unit at the Veterans Administration Healthcare Center writes in a 2011 article that "in the past 15 years, new evidence has emerged from 7

> *"Many kids get high not to stay low."*[61]
>
> — Oscar Bukstein, associate professor of psychiatry at the University of Pittsburgh School of Medicine.

Animal Studies

Because marijuana has never been the focus of a broad-based clinical trial, many of marijuana's side effects have been largely unstudied. Evidence from a small number of animal studies, however, suggests physical and psychological side effects that may preclude its use for certain conditions. These studies have confirmed, for example, that cannabis may increase the risk of bleeding or may cause low blood pressure.

In addition, some studies seem to indicate that marijuana is involved in producing a fear, or paranoid, response. In experiments on rats, researchers found certain cannabinoid receptors are activated by THC, the main psychoactive substance of marijuana. When rats were given a shock after their cannabinoid receptors had been stimulated, they would freeze in fear. Scientists concluded that marijuana can lead the brain to "jump to conclusions about mild experiences involving particular places or things, and to perceive them as scarier and more strongly connected than they are." Such conclusions indicate that the paranoia that accompanies some marijuana users' experiences is well-founded in animal research.

Maia Szalavitz, "Why Pot Smokers Are Paranoid," *Time*, April 4, 2011. http://healthland.time.com.

. . . studies that cumulatively provide strong support for an association between cannabis use as an adolescent or young adult and a greater risk for developing a psychotic disorder such as schizophrenia." Although Pierre concedes that "a causal relationship has not been firmly established," he concludes that "current evidence supports that cannabis is a 'component' cause of chronic psychosis."[63]

However, marijuana seems to have the opposite effect on some individuals, leading to further confusion over whether marijuana has detrimental long-term effects on mental health. A small body of research indicates that marijuana may have some protective effects. Neuropsychologist John Stirling and his team at the Research Institute for Health and Social Change at Manchester Metropolitan University recorded cannabis use among 112 admitted mental patients (mostly schizophrenic). When these patients were followed up 10 to 12 years later, researchers found that the marijuana users had better cognitive function in several areas, including verbal fluency and face recognition memory. Clearly, marijuana's effect on serious mental disorders requires further study before definitive conclusions can be drawn. In the years ahead, scientists, government officials, and medical professionals will continue to study these and other issues in an attempt to ascertain how medical marijuana impacts health and society.

Facts

- NIDA has declared that marijuana has no permanent, negative effect on human reproductive systems.

- According to NIDA, brain imaging studies in chronic marijuana users show consistent alterations, although the connection to impaired cognitive functioning remains uncertain.

- The National Academy of Sciences reports that several studies associate workers who smoke marijuana with increased absences, tardiness, accidents, workers' compensation claims, and job turnover.

- A study at NYU School of Medicine suggests that smoking marijuana may be associated with conflicts in personal relationships.

- According to Leslie Iverson, a pharmacology professor at Cambridge University, between 10 and 30 percent of marijuana users develop dependency.

Can Medical Marijuana Improve Mental Health?

While medical marijuana is being used to treat many physical diseases, its use in treating various mental disorders is also being studied. An arsenal of drugs has been discovered in the last 20 years to treat such disorders as depression, schizophrenia, and, most recently, PTSD, but not all of these medications work for everyone. Some people who cannot tolerate the side effects of current medicines or find that their symptoms persist say they have found relief with marijuana. Marijuana has long been used to elevate mood and reduce stress and anxiety. In the laboratory, researchers have duplicated these results, proving that cannabinoids stimulate the pleasure centers in the brain.

Physicians currently recommending marijuana to some of their patients are finding it alleviates many of their symptoms. According to the physicians affiliated with the organization Cannabis Healing, which supports the medical use of marijuana to treat a variety of conditions:

> Cannabis has proven to be a highly effective treatment for anxiety, depression, bipolar disorder, insomnia, anger management, and attention deficit disorder. Most physi-

cians with sizable numbers of cannabis patients report that about twenty five percent of their patients use cannabis for one of the above conditions. Cannabis is often reported to be more effective than prescription medications but is often used in conjunction with them. Approximately half the patients use only cannabis. The remaining half nearly always is able to reduce the number and/or the doses of prescription medications.[64]

Depression

The use of marijuana in treating depression seems especially promising for some patients. Depression is a serious mental disorder characterized by many well-documented symptoms. The most common symptoms include a sense of overwhelming sadness and doom, a loss of energy, changes in appetite and sleep patterns, obsession over past losses, and difficulty concentrating and thinking. Depression can occur on its own or accompany a long illness, such as during the rigors of cancer treatment.

As George McMahon, a patient who received marijuana as part of the US government's Investigational New Drug Program, describes it: "People who have never struggled with a life threatening or disabling illness often do not comprehend how debilitating the resulting depression can be. Long days spent struggling with sickness can wear patients down, suppress their appetites and slowly destroy their wills to live. The psychological damage can result in physiological effects that may be the difference between living and dying."[65]

According to Igor Grant, cannabis can treat multiple symptoms of a debilitating illness, eliminating the need for several medications. For many patients, marijuana's ability to reduce the number and amount of other medications is especially appealing. Cannabis is a good painkiller, but it also imparts a sense of well-being and so addresses the sense of defeat that may come with a long-term illness. As one physician explains: "In the case of pain, it's actually difficult to disentangle the pain relief from the emotional components of pain. An argument could be

> "Cannabis has proven to be a highly effective treatment for anxiety, depression, bipolar disorder, insomnia, anger management, and attention deficit disorder."[64]
>
> — Cannabis Healing, a medical marijuana advocacy group.

made that if you're a person with terminal cancer, maybe it's OK to blunt your mood or change your mood in a certain direction. The anti-anxiety and anti-pain effect work together to produce a positive action."[66]

Donald Abrams, a cancer doctor, also admits that part of the reason he recommends marijuana to his cancer patients is that it can alleviate depression and insomnia in addition to the nausea, pain, and loss of appetite associated with the disease.

Other doctors concur that using marijuana to treat pain has many additional benefits. In his article "Implementation of the Compassionate Use Act in a Family Medical Practice: Seven Years Clinical Experience," physician Frank Lucido contends that he uses cannabis to treat mental anguish, including anxiety or depression, as well as physical symptoms: "With appropriate use of medical cannabis, many of these patients have been able to reduce or eliminate the use of opiates and other pain pills, ritalin, tranquilizers, sleeping pills, anti-depressants and other psychiatric medicines. . . . Symptoms [treated] include, but are not limited to: fatigue, insomnia, depression, anxiety, nausea, vomiting, anorexia, elimination problems, and breathing difficulty."[67]

A Mood-Brightening Effect?

A body of research appears to corroborate these anecdotal reports, suggesting that the cannabinoids in marijuana may have a positive effect on patients suffering depression. In particular, a study by Kurt Blaas, a doctor in Austria, shows promise. In Austria, a chemical form of THC (the active psychotropic drug in marijuana), called dronabinol, is available by prescription. Blaas used dronabinol to treat depressed patients who had not been helped by traditional antidepressants. Between 2003 and 2006 Blaas treated 250 patients with dronabinol. Some 75 of these patients, or 30 percent, suffered from depression, a chronic sense of feeling overwhelmed or exhausted. The results were overwhelmingly positive. As Blaas writes: "For about almost 80% of patients, use of the medication related with swift improvement of the depressed mood or the sense of being overwhelmed. Only 20% of patients did not experience any significant mood brightening."[68] Even for these patients, however, the effects of dronabinol were enhanced when Blaas added a traditional antidepressant.

In one case, a 48-year-old woman had had a record of depression, aggravated by a continued addiction to alcohol and drugs. At the start, the woman suffered from severe depression following the death of her father. Blaas treated the woman over a six-year period. While on dronabinol, she was able to quit drinking and using drugs. She reported that "her quality of life was greatly improved."[69] Her chronic episodes of depression, when they did occur, were far less severe and did not lead into her previous drug and alcohol abuse.

While Blaas was able to openly use a legal form of marijuana to treat his patients, research on mood disorders in the United States is more complicated because of the banning of the substance. In another study performed at the University of Texas at Austin by Regina A. Mangieri, rats were used to research the effects of cannabinoids. Rats were first forced to undergo various stresses to make them suffer symptoms of depression. Mangieri concluded that cannabinoids appeared to produce effects similar to those observed following other antidepressant treatments.

"Using marijuana can worsen depression and lead to more serious mental health disorders, such as schizophrenia, anxiety, and even suicide."[70]

— Office of National Drug Control Policy.

Contradictory Evidence

In stark contrast, others contend that far from alleviating depression or other disorders, marijuana causes, or at least contributes to them, especially in teens. An analysis by the Office of National Drug Control Policy concludes that "studies show that marijuana and depression are a dangerous combination. In fact, using marijuana can worsen depression and lead to more serious mental health disorders, such as schizophrenia, anxiety, and even suicide. Weekly or more frequent use of marijuana doubles a teen's risk of depression and anxiety."[70] Similarly, a study published in the journal *Addiction* showed that marijuana use was associated with depression and suicide.

Margaret Trudeau, the ex-wife of Canada's former prime minister, has publicly discussed her use of marijuana and its harmful effect on her mental health. Trudeau, who suffered for years with mental illness, says giving up marijuana has been an important part of her recovery.

Anecdotal evidence that marijuana exacerbates symptoms does exist. Margaret Trudeau, ex-wife of former Canadian prime minister Pierre Trudeau, agrees that marijuana has a negative effect on mental health and not vice versa: "Quitting cannabis has been an important part of my recovery from mental illness. Marijuana can trigger psychosis. Every time I was hospitalized it was preceded by heavy marijuana use."[71]

In addition, some evidence suggests that dosage may make a significant difference in the effectiveness of marijuana, something that has always been difficult to monitor since the drug is smoked and comes in different potencies. During a study published in the October 24, 2007, issue of the *Journal of Neuroscience*, a low dose of cannabinoid elevated laboratory rats' mood, while more undid the benefits. As researcher Gabriella Gobbi of McGill University explains, "Excessive cannabis use in people with depression poses high risk of psychosis."[72]

Anxiety and Mood Disorders

Related to depression are other mood disorders such as chronic anxiety and bipolar disorder, and both of these illnesses have been fodder for medical marijuana. In the case of chronic anxiety, much of the evidence remains anecdotal and mixed. For some, marijuana is a vast improvement over conventional anxiety medication. In an article in *Elle* magazine, Patsy K. Eagan chronicles a lifetime of coping with generalized anxiety disorder. Treated with conventional medications as a teen and young adult, Eagan found that she experienced relief, but only for a short time. Those medications eventually led her to have panic attacks. She switched to others but experienced side effects such as irrational bouts of anger: "Surges of elation or rage would seize me at work while I was doing mundane tasks, like shelving. Once, I almost threw a punch at one of the regular, but by no means normal, customers. . . . After a few of these episodes, it became clear that there was no peace for me in Paxil [one of the prescribed drugs]. Calm came, I found, only from pot."[73]

Another patient found that he could not tolerate the side effects of traditional medicines. Describing the effects of the prescription drugs that he took to treat his pain and depression, he claims, "The side effects of these drugs ran the gamut from constipation and stomach ulcers to erectile dysfunction and addiction. The extreme pain coupled with the drugs led to my anxiety and depression." After trying marijuana, he proclaimed: "It worked. I was able to cut out four of the prescription meds. . . . It relieves my anxiety and I am not depressed. If I actually took all the medications they prescribed me, I would be a vegetable. Today, I am motivated to get things done and to live my life."[74]

"Quitting cannabis has been an important part of my recovery from mental illness. Marijuana can trigger psychosis. Every time I was hospitalized it was preceded by heavy marijuana use."[71]

— Margaret Trudeau, ex-wife of former Canadian prime minister Pierre Trudeau.

Bipolar Disorder

In the case of bipolar disorder, major depression alternates with uncontrollable mania, or elation. Traditional treatments for the disorder include lithium salts and anticonvulsant drugs, which can have serious side effects. Of bipolar patients, 30 to 40 percent report not being helped by current medications. Again, evidence that marijuana can ease the symptoms of bipolar disorder remains anecdotal. In an article published in the *Journal of Psychoactive Drugs*, physician Lester Grinspoon relates the case of a bipolar woman who had battled her symptoms for years. Unable to tolerate the side effects of lithium, the woman began using marijuana. She claims: "Suppose I am in a fit of manic rage—the most destructive behavior of all. A few puffs of this [marijuana] and I can be calm. My husband and I have both noticed this: it is quite dramatic. One minute out of control in a mad rage over a meaningless detail seemingly in need of a strait jacket. . . . Then, within a few minutes, the time it takes to smoke a few pinches—why, I could even, after a round of apologies, laugh at myself!" Although there is no cure for bipolar disorder, as this woman acknowledges, she concludes that "Cannabis lessens what is troubling me and returns me to a more normal state."[75]

A number of doctors who use marijuana to treat their bipolar patients report that the drug effectively treats some of the symptoms of the disease. Physician Jay Cavanaugh says that while cannabis cannot yet be considered a primary treatment, it brightens patients' mood and significantly reduces the severity of both manic and depressive states, especially when combined with traditional treatments:

> Numerous patients report significant improvement and stabilization with their bipolar disorder when they utilize adjunctive [additional] therapy with medical cannabis. While some mental health professionals worry about the impact of cannabis on aggravating manic states, most bipolar patients trying cannabis find they "cycle" less often and find

"Cannabis lessens what is troubling me and returns me to a more normal state."[75]

— A woman who uses marijuana to alleviate symptoms of bipolar disorder.

Marijuana and ADHD

Author Christopher Largen describes how marijuana alleviated his symptoms of attention-deficit/hyperactivity disorder (ADHD) at a young age:

> I am the youngest therapeutic cannabis user on record in the United States. I smoked my first joint in 1971, when I was two years old. . . . I was constantly screaming and crying, destroying property, and aggressing toward other people. . . . When I bit my preschool teacher on the leg and smashed my fist through the living room window, my parents became desperate. . . .
>
> My parents were Southerners. They knew folk remedies, like rubbing sweet rum on the swollen gums of teething babies. They thought cannabis wouldn't harm me, and they suspected it might relax me. The held the joint to my lips, telling me to suck it like a straw. . . .
>
> Mom and Dad were amazed by the results. The marijuana curbed my aggression, reduced my tantrums, elevated my mood, increased my appetite, and helped me sleep.

Christopher Largen, "I'm the Youngest Marijuana User on Record in the U.S.," *Illegal Blog*, October 25, 2005. http://waronjunk.blogspot.com.

significant improvement in overall mood. Bipolar disorders vary tremendously in the time spent in the depressive versus manic states. Those who experience extended depressive episodes are more likely to be helped with cannabis.[76]

Cavanaugh and other advocates believe that marijuana can help bipolar patients lead more normal and productive lives.

As a treatment for this serious disorder, however, some evidence suggests that marijuana can aggravate symptoms. In some individuals cannabis can actually increase psychosis. It can also provoke the manic state in some bipolar sufferers, or interfere with traditional medications when sufferers are using both. Yet this conclusion, too, remains controversial because many bipolar sufferers go years before they are diagnosed. They may in fact have been using marijuana for years to quell symptoms. By the time they are diagnosed, physicians may wrongly assume that the marijuana use may have propelled the disease. "Teens and adults with bipolar disorder are the most self-medicating emotional disorder group, often turning to drugs and alcohol to quell their mood swings,"[77] comments Nicole Gregston, a case manager with Mental Health and Mental Retardation (MHMR) in Austin, Texas.

This chicken-or-egg effect seems clearer among long-term marijuana users. An extensive analysis of studies of marijuana use and mental illness later in life suggests that the risk of developing serious mental disorders among heavy marijuana users was 40 percent. The increase in psychosis was even greater, anywhere from 50 to 200 percent. The dangers are significant for those that begin marijuana use as teens. In an article published in the British medical journal the *Lancet* in 2007, researchers conclude: "There is now sufficient evidence to warn young people that using cannabis could increase their risk of developing a psychotic illness later in life."[78]

Post-Traumatic Stress Disorder

While the perils of marijuana's effects on memory have been lampooned in popular media for decades, this very property may prove useful in treating people who suffer from not being able to forget psychological trauma. Those who suffer from PTSD—debilitating levels of anxiety that usually follow prolonged periods of exposure to stress such as in war or prolonged sexual abuse or violence—may be helped by marijuana's ability to dull memory.

Since the Vietnam War, veterans have self-medicated with marijuana to ease symptoms of PTSD, including unprovoked rage and fear as well as nightmares and night sweats. Paul Culkin, who suffers from PTSD after serving in Kosovo in 2004 as part of an

army bomb squad, was constantly exposed to danger. Though his injury from a car bomb led to his honorable discharge, Culkin continues to experience the psychological effects of the war. "Sometimes you'll see a car that's just not in the right place and it'll send me back to that thinking that it could, possibly, be a car bomb."[79]

Though Culkin found relief in traditional psychiatric treatment with counseling and antidepressants, he was still, on occasion, overwhelmed with anxiety. After becoming part of a New Mexico state program to test the effects of medical marijuana on alleviating the symptoms of PTSD, Culkin says that marijuana has greatly improved his anxiety. His wife reports that "he's a different person. He's a better person. He's more open. He's more communicative. At one point, we almost got a divorce, and I can honestly say that I think medical cannabis saved our marriage and our family."[80]

A 2012 study published in the journal *Neuropsychopharmacology* reported that rats that had been exposed to "severe, Navy Seal–

US Marines in Afghanistan evacuate a wounded comrade. Some members of the military who suffer from post-traumatic stress disorder have turned to marijuana to dull the painful and traumatic memories of war and ease symptoms such as sudden rage, nightmares, and night sweats.

level stress, including restraint, forced swims, and anesthetization" showed symptoms of traumatic stress similar to humans. Researchers found that "rats that were severely stressed, then immediately given a synthetic compound that mimics the effects of THC . . . were mellower. They showed none of the stress-related changes seen in the rats receiving placebo."[81]

Many in the medical community are skeptical of such reports. As David Speigel, director of the Stanford Center on Stress and Health, opines: "There is no solid evidence that cannabinoids—that marijuana—is, in itself, an effective treatment for post-traumatic stress disorder. . . . Before anyone can claim that, there needs to be some more solid research on that topic."[82]

Such research may be on the way. According to the Multidisciplinary Association for Psychedelic Studies (MAPS), many US veterans will continue to use marijuana to effectively treat their symptoms of PTSD. The FDA recently accepted the organization's plans to conduct a human study to scientifically assess the effectiveness of marijuana for symptoms of PTSD in war veterans. The study is pending additional approval by the National Institute on Drug Abuse and the Public Health Service.

Attention-Deficit/Hyperactivity Disorder

Attention-deficit/hyperactivity disorder (ADHD) affects many children and adults. Those with ADHD experience an inability to focus on tasks. For some adolescents, the symptoms are so severe that they are unable to pay attention in class or focus on their homework or other studies. When symptoms persist into adulthood, many can neither hold down jobs nor lead productive lives. Family practitioner Marian Fry is just one of many physicians who believe that medical marijuana may help with the disorder. While 85 percent of her patients use marijuana to treat chronic pain, 15 percent use it to treat psychiatric disorders, including ADHD. According to Fry: "Most ADHD patients in my practice are teenagers with parental consent to substitute Cannabis for more dangerous and addicting drugs like Ritalin, Dexedrine, etc. These patients do much better with Cannabis, show marked improvement in appetite and sleep, and are more successful in school."[83]

Pediatrician Seth Ammerman firmly disagrees. Writing in the 2011 issue of *California Pediatrician*, Ammerman says, "There are anecdotal reports of the successful use of medical marijuana by adolescents for the treatment of a variety of health conditions, ranging from attention deficit disorder to anxiety and depression to autism. . . . There are no published studies on the use of medical marijuana in the pediatric or adolescent patient populations. . . .

Marijuana and Depression

A supporter of medical marijuana reports how marijuana helps him deal with depression related to chronic pain:

Due to service-related injuries in the U.S. Navy, I suffer from chronic pain in my back, legs, and chest, which has left me incapable of performing many average everyday functions, which in turn has caused severe depression. . . . Marijuana allows me to focus my mind somewhere other than my back pain. Instead of wondering how much relief chewing my right leg off will provide, I can focus on the positive things in my life, like my wife and child. Relief from depression is where marijuana really helps me most. Living in endless pain can make you feel very hopeless. For most of my life I was proud of my body; I was fit and able to stand up straight and tall. Today that isn't the case. Marijuana provides safer relief from my chronic pain and allows me to be an active participant in my own life once again.

Quoted in Mickey Martin, *Medical Marijuana 101*. Oakland, CA: Quick American, 2011, pp. 30–31.

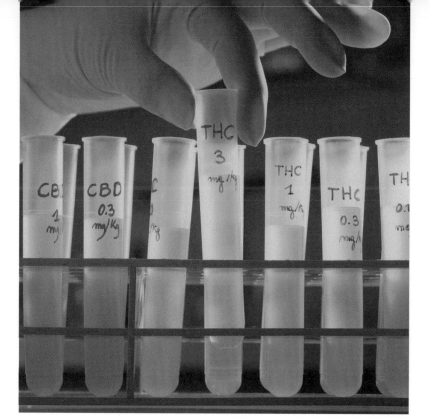

Test tubes containing compounds found in cannabis are used in research. The medicinal effects of these compounds are being studied on a wide array of mental illnesses, neurological disorders, and physical ailments.

Thus there are no current data available to support the prescribing of medical marijuana for adolescents."[84] Ammerman goes on to say that adolescent brain maturation does not occur until the early- to mid-twenties, and so marijuana use may alter the developing brain in ways not fully understood. In addition, some studies have found an uptick in depression and suicide among teens who chronically use marijuana.

Other Disorders

Some of the chemical substances in marijuana imitate naturally occurring substances in the body. By studying marijuana, scientists hope to unlock the secrets of the role some of these chemicals play in diseases and disorders that have not, so far, yielded to medical solutions.

For example, Tourette's syndrome is a disorder characterized by an array of behavioral and cognitive disorders, and, most notably, motor and verbal tics. A chemical called anandamide, found naturally in the body, helps control body movement and coordination and is also chemically similar to marijuana. Researcher Daniele Piomelli, an associate professor of pharmacology at the University of California at Irvine, has been studying Tourette's syndrome and similar disorders for over a decade. His research focuses on how anandamides work in the brain to produce normal movement. According to Piomelli, "By understanding how the anandamide system works similarly to marijuana, we can explore new ways to treat these diseases more effectively."[85] This ongoing research may be the key to treating other, similar diseases that involve the anandamide system, such as schizophrenia.

Schizophrenia, a disease in which sufferers experience paranoia and auditory and visual hallucinations, is a mysterious disorder that is currently treated with heavy-duty antipsychotics that have a variety of side effects. Dealing with these side effects along with their paranoia causes many schizophrenics to refuse to take the medication. Schizophrenia affects about 1.1 percent of the population. Researchers have discovered some evidence that schizophrenics may have higher levels of anandamide. Scientists surmise that the body may produce higher levels of anandamide to counteract the symptoms, acting as a natural antipsychotic. Indeed, those suffering with schizophrenia or similar mental disorders have reported that marijuana alleviates their symptoms.

Cannabidinol may also play a role in the alleviation of schizophrenic symptoms. A team of researchers in Brazil documented that cannabidinol may have antipsychotic properties. Although the research is still in its infancy, results from preclinical and clinical studies suggest that cannabidinol may prove to be a safe, well-tolerated alternative treatment for schizophrenic patients, though why the treatment works is not completely understood. Equally baffling, a number of studies suggest that marijuana actually causes schizophrenia and other psychotic disorders.

Important Role in Research

The promise held by cannabidinol, however, seems to crop up in the treatment of many mood and behavior disorders. It has even been found useful in the treatment of another persistent problem, cocaine addiction. Cannabidinol seems to activate a receptor that reduces the impulse to use cocaine. The hope is that scientists can isolate and synthesize the chemical that seems to stimulate the anti-addiction receptor to treat cocaine and other addictions.

Mood disorders are perhaps the most mysterious and most misunderstood group of diseases, mostly because they involve the brain and body chemistry in complex ways. Scientists continue to hope that understanding the naturally occurring chemicals in the body and their roles in disease will further improve their understanding of these processes and their roles in mood disorders. Marijuana's role in studying these chemicals is, at the moment, an important part of that research.

Facts

- A 2012 paper published by the independent research institute IZA suggests that the passage of a law legalizing the use of marijuana for medical purposes is associated with an almost 5 percent drop in a state's suicide rate.

- The ONDCP reports that depressed teens are more than twice as likely as their peers to use marijuana.

- Data from California dispensaries suggest that the number of people who use medical marijuana for psychological disorders is rising.

- With so many strains of marijuana—each with a unique chemical composition—users can have difficulty finding the strain that will produce the most positive, therapeutic effect.

- A 2007 study in the *Journal of Neuroscience* reported that patients who used medical marijuana to treat symptoms of AIDS or multiple sclerosis showed a significant improvement in mood disorders.

How Should the Medical Use of Marijuana Be Regulated?

Medical marijuana is, in some ways, in legal limbo between state and federal laws. Federal law is clear-cut on marijuana: It is illegal, it is dangerous, and anyone who possesses or sells the substance can be prosecuted under the law. State laws are not so clear-cut. While some states comply with federal law, others have legalized marijuana through voter referenda. These laws vary from state to state. While these states all recognize medical marijuana as legal, they vary in how and by whom the substance can be prescribed, who can grow it, and where it can be purchased. So, in states that allow medical marijuana, patients, dispensaries, and growers are sometimes caught between federal and state laws. As late as July 2011 the federal government reaffirmed its ruling that marijuana has no accepted medical use and should have the same classification as highly dangerous drugs such as heroin. Yet voters have refused to accept the government's position, especially when it comes to medical marijuana.

The 2011 decision seemed unreasonable to many involved in the marijuana issue, especially because the drug's status and acceptance seems to have changed so drastically since the federal government first classified marijuana in 1970. Sixteen states have legalized medical marijuana, including Alaska, Arizona, California, Colorado, Delaware, Hawaii, Maine, Michigan, Montana, Nevada, New Jersey, New Mexico, Oregon, Vermont, Washington, and Rhode Island, as well as the District of Columbia. Studies have been done that indicate it is of benefit in the treatment of some physical and mental conditions. When the ruling was announced, DEA administrator Michele M. Leonhart argued that the federal government was justified in its determination not to accept marijuana as a medicine, because "its chemistry is not known and studies have not been done on its usefulness or safety. . . . At this time the known risks of marijuana use have not been shown to be outweighed by specific benefits in well-controlled clinical trials that scientifically evaluate safety and efficacy."[86] Advocates in the medical marijuana debate found this renewed stance disappointing.

Federal and State Laws Collide

Many of these supporters contend that the federal government is wrong to have taken such a strong stance when so many states have passed laws legalizing medical marijuana. This mismatch between state and federal law makes obtaining medical marijuana complicated for patients who want to take advantage of the state laws. Medical marijuana laws vary in each state. In some states patients can legally grow their own marijuana, while in others they cannot. The amount of marijuana a patient can possess and whether dispensaries can legally sell marijuana also varies by state. Although all of the laws essentially protect qualified patients from arrest for using marijuana to alleviate certain medical conditions when done so under the advice of a physician, obtaining the substance legally can be a problem.

The state governments do not run the marijuana business. Marijuana is not grown on state-run farms, nor is it dispensed by state-run facilities. Rather, private marijuana growers sell to qualified dispensaries or patients in their area, which complies with federal laws that govern interstate and in-

"At this time the known risks of marijuana use have not been shown to be outweighed by specific benefits in well-controlled clinical trials that scientifically evaluate safety and efficacy."[86]

— DEA administrator Michele M. Leonhart.

tercity commerce. So state governments do not come into direct conflict with federal law. State laws simply determine not to arrest patients who acquire their own medicine through privately run marijuana businesses.

At the same time, federal law renders marijuana possession illegal, so patients may still be subject to federal prosecution for possession or cultivation of marijuana. For example, baggage screeners at airports work for the Transportation Security Administration, a federal agency, and so may turn medical marijuana patients over to police for prosecution, even if state law deems the marijuana use legal. Likewise, border patrol officers are charged with enforcing federal law and can therefore arrest medical marijuana patients,

Agents from the US Drug Enforcement Administration remove marijuana plants from a San Francisco medical marijuana dispensary. Citing violations of federal law, agents raided dispensaries in 2011 and 2012. Seized plants were destroyed and dispensaries and growers forced to close down.

The Medical Marijuana Dispensary

A paper published by the California Police Chiefs Association illustrates how a typical marijuana dispensary operates:

> A guard or employee may check for medical marijuana cards or physician recommendations at the entrance. Many types and grades of marijuana are usually available. Although employees are neither pharmacists nor doctors, sales clerks will probably make recommendations about what type of marijuana will best relieve a given medical symptom. Baked goods containing marijuana may be available and sold, although there is usually no health permit to sell baked goods. The dispensary will give the patient a form to sign declaring that the dispensary is their "primary caregiver" (a process fraught with legal difficulties). The patient then selects the marijuana desired and is told what the "contribution" will be for the product. The California Health & Safety Code specifically prohibits the sale of marijuana to a patient, so "contributions" are made to reimburse the dispensary for its time and care in making the "product" available.

California Police Chiefs Association's Task Force on Marijuana Dispensaries, "White Paper on Marijuana Dispensaries," 2009, p. 7.

even those who have obtained their marijuana in accordance with state law. Because the vast majority of marijuana prosecutions are made at the state level, however, most of the state laws are fairly effective in protecting patients who choose to use medical marijuana—and the physicians who recommend it.

Where and how patients obtain marijuana are different matters. Even when home growing and dispensaries are legal by state law, the federal government can decide that they are not complying with federal guidelines. The federal government continues to find reasons to raid marijuana dispensaries in some states, such as California, Colorado, and Oregon. In 2011 and 2012 the DEA destroyed plants, seized property, and closed growers and dispensaries that it argued violated federal law.

When former US attorney Joseph Russoniello was asked about recent raids in California, he explained that dispensaries were violating federal regulations, such as dispensing marijuana beyond their own jurisdictions. He claims the raids were justified:

> I think that the U.S. attorneys would probably agree that about 96 to 98 percent of all of the operators and all the dispensaries certainly in the state were out of compliance with the state guidelines, because they were commercial enterprises, because, you know, they were not limiting themselves to people who lived within their jurisdiction. As soon as you start crossing the county lines and start packaging it and sort of suggesting that your client base or your patients, or your members, really, are all over the state, you're basically in a commercial enterprise for profit.[87]

Many of these growers and dispensaries disagreed with Russoniello and are facing court battles to show that they were in compliance with state and federal guidelines. One grower who complies with state and federal guidelines, Matthew Cohen, thinks that the federal government simply wants the dispensaries to go away: "It certainly sends the message that the federal government would prefer that . . . [marijuana providers] operate underground, unregulated."[88]

Marijuana Dispensaries

While advocates argue that the growers and dispensaries are victims of the legal tangle between state and federal laws, detractors claim the industry is a front to sell marijuana to whomever wants it. Though most states regulate where dispensaries can operate, most communities find the dispensaries distasteful and argue that they attract other businesses such as tattoo parlors and porn shops that are equally distasteful. In California, 185 cities and counties banned pot dispensaries entirely. In New Jersey, rules on where dispensaries can locate are so restrictive that operating a dispensary there is virtually impossible. So, while medically needy patients can receive a prescription for marijuana in these states, they may still have difficulty in obtaining it. And these problems will be difficult to solve because the federal government and the states have different laws.

Igor Grant argues that this classic catch-22 situation—whereby physicians may recommend medical marijuana according to state law, but patients are unable to obtain it through legal channels because of federal prohibitions—should be revamped. He says,

> I think if the research confirms what we believe to be true, that the marijuana or the constituents of marijuana can be medically helpful in several diseases, then we have an obligation to make these things available to patients who need it. And the question then becomes how do we do that? I think the present system with dispensaries and people trying to get marijuana on the street wherever they can is not a good medical model. . . . You wouldn't want to buy pills for any other condition on the street, not knowing what's in them. So we need to get to a point where if cannabis is prescribed, in whatever form, that the patients can be assured of their purity and potency, just like we would expect with any medicine.[89]

Since the first medical marijuana law passed in California in 1996, how marijuana should be regulated to mitigate concerns remains unsolved. Even though polls have found that the vast majority of Americans—77 percent, according to one 2011 CBS News poll—approve of legalized medical marijuana, they may also suffer from a "not in my backyard" attitude when it comes to having it bought and sold in their communities.

Influences on Teen Marijuana Use

While only a minority of states have legalized medical marijuana, many people believe that these laws simply endorse its recreational use, especially among young people. These fears can be reviewed empirically in statistics from states that have legalized marijuana. Studies that have looked at marijuana use in California, Oregon, and Colorado show that nonmedical marijuana use did not increase after passage of medical marijuana laws.

Numerous studies compare states that have legalized marijuana with states with similar demographics that have not made marijuana legal. One study compared Rhode Island, which legalized marijuana, with Massachusetts, which did not. Esther Choo, assistant professor of emergency medicine at Brown University and leader of the study, states that the comparison was apt: "We wanted to pair these two states because they have so much in common culturally and geographically."[90] Choo used data collected from the Centers for Disease Control and Prevention from 1997 to 2009. The study involved about 13,000 teens in Rhode Island and 25,000 teens in Massachusetts. The study concluded that in any given year, 30 percent of the teens had used marijuana within the previous month. So, although marijuana use was common among teens, its legal status had little effect on teen use. Choo thinks that the population that uses medical marijuana, usually very sick adults, does not inspire its use among teens: "Whether they are taking it for pain or for vomiting control or appetite, this is not a group we think of as superinspiring for young people to take up their drug pattern."[91]

Other research confirms Choo's findings. A study conducted by Mitch Earleywine, associate professor of psychology at the State University of New York, Albany, compared teen marijuana use before (1996) and after (2004) California passed its medical marijuana law. Among ninth graders, previous month pot smoking had declined by 47 percent. Earleywine said, "Nearly 15 years after the passage of the nation's first state medical marijuana law, California's Prop. 215, a considerable body of data shows that teens' marijuana use has generally gone down following the passage of medical marijuana laws."[92] Like other researchers who have studied the issue, Earleywine argues that the ill people who use medical marijuana do not inspire young people to want to use the drug.

"A considerable body of data shows that teens' marijuana use has generally gone down following the passage of medical marijuana laws."[92]

— Mitch Earleywine, associate professor of psychology at the State University of New York.

Obtaining Prescriptions

Not just increased teen use concerns medical marijuana detractors. Many fear that legalizing marijuana in any form will inevitably lead to widespread use and even attempts to legalize it for recreational use. Some argue this is already happening. Doctors accept payment to write anyone a prescription, many argue, and even people with vague complaints who are not seriously ill can obtain a prescription easily. For example, the Department of Community Health in Michigan reported in 2011 that most medical marijuana patients in the state were obtaining certification to use marijuana for nonspecific ailments such as pain and nausea, as opposed to more specific, serious conditions like cancer. Opponents charge that many of these patients who procure marijuana under the guise of a nonspecific ailment are just using the marijuana for recreational purposes.

In fact, some states do seem to be more lenient than others as to what can qualify a person for legal use. All legal medical marijuana states approve such conditions as cancer, AIDS, chronic pain, severe nausea, and uncontrolled muscle spasms, and each

Marijuana grows in the window of a coffee shop in the Dutch city of Amsterdam. Marijuana is openly sold in the Netherlands, where authorities believe that legalization leads to less illegal activity and less use of hard drugs.

allows for the state health department to approve other conditions. But in some states, such as California, for example, doctors have even more discretion. The state law allows marijuana to be prescribed for any other illness for which marijuana provides relief. This type of leniency, detractors claim, leads to widespread marijuana use.

Yet all states where medical marijuana is legal, except Washington and Maryland, require patients to receive a medical identification card issued by the state's health department or regulatory agency. These can only be obtained after a physician has recommended the patient for marijuana. Proponents argue that these laws continue to prevent marijuana's widespread use and cite drug arrests as evidence. For example, since the passage of Prop. 215 in California, 74,000 arrests have been made for illegal marijuana possession. Clearly, many are still being prosecuted for illegal use.

Gateway to Harder Drugs

In addition to wider use, many believe that once medical marijuana is legalized and its use is more accepted, it will become a gateway to the use of harder drugs. The US government has consistently noted this as one reason for its hard line on the drug. One piece of evidence frequently cited for this theory is that when interviewed, many hard-core drug addicts will say that they started with marijuana. According to the National Institute on Drug Abuse, pot users are 104 times more likely to use cocaine than are those who have never tried pot.

However, studies have failed to confirm this idea. Even federally funded studies of drug use have not been able to prove the connection. In 2009, for example, 2.3 million people reported using marijuana, while only 617,000 had used cocaine and 180,000 had tried heroin. Legalization proponents argue that the connection is a false one because marijuana is simply the most widely used illegal drug, and so it is the one that people are most likely to encounter.

Others cite the Netherlands and Portugal as examples—in these countries, where marijuana is legal and widely accepted, higher rates of abuse of other illicit drugs have not been found. The Netherlands, for example, adheres to a policy of separating

The Current Debate

The Congressional Research Service (CRS) is the organization charged with providing analysis and commentary of federal and state policies on a variety of issues that are put under congressional review. In their 2010 report regarding marijuana policies, the CRS describes the issues that will continue to inform the debate in the years ahead:

> Claims and counterclaims about medical marijuana—much debated by journalists and academics, policymakers at all levels of government, and interested citizens—include the following: Marijuana is harmful and has no medical value; marijuana effectively treats the symptoms of certain diseases; smoking is an improper route of drug administration; marijuana should be rescheduled to permit medical use; state medical marijuana laws send the wrong message and lead to increased illicit drug use; the medical marijuana movement undermines the war on drugs; patients should not be arrested for using medical marijuana; the federal government should allow the states to experiment and should not interfere with state medical marijuana programs; medical marijuana laws harm the federal drug approval process; the medical cannabis movement is a cynical ploy to legalize marijuana and other drugs. With strong opinions being expressed on all sides of this complex issue, the debate over medical marijuana does not appear to be approaching resolution.

Congressional Research Service, *Medical Marijuana: Review and Analysis of Federal and State Policies*, April 2, 2010. www.fas.org.

the market for hard-core drugs, such as heroin, from a relatively "soft" drug, such as marijuana, which is openly sold in many coffee shops. Dutch authorities believe that by legalizing marijuana and making it widely accessible, users are less likely to purchase it from an illegal source that might also sell hard drugs. It is difficult to quantify this claim, however, since Dutch citizens, in general, seem to use all drugs, including marijuana, far less than their counterparts in the United States and the rest of Europe.

Violence and Crime

Detractors and proponents of medical marijuana do not have to go across the ocean to confirm statistics. The state of California may be the most heavily studied place to determine whether marijuana has had a negative impact on society. One of the most scrutinized issues is whether medical marijuana's legalization has increased crime—especially in the areas where dispensaries are located. The Los Angeles Police Department has continuously argued that crime around neighborhoods with dispensaries has risen. According to a 2009 white paper published by the California Police Chiefs Association's Task Force on Marijuana Dispensaries, marijuana has increased burglary, murder, organized crime, poisonings, and other serious crimes. The paper states:

> *"Marijuana storefront businesses have allowed criminals to flourish in California."*[93]
>
> — California Police Chiefs Association's Task Force on Marijuana Dispensaries.

Marijuana storefront businesses have allowed criminals to flourish in California. In the summer of 2007, the City of San Diego cooperated with federal authorities and served search warrants on several marijuana dispensary locations. In addition to marijuana, many weapons were recovered, including a stolen handgun and an M-16 assault rifle. The National Drug Intelligence Center reports that marijuana growers are employing armed guards, using explosive booby traps, and murdering people to shield their crops. Street gangs of all national origins are involved in transporting and distributing marijuana to meet the ever increasing demand for the drug. Active Asian gangs have included members of Vietnamese organized crime syndicates who have migrated from Canada to buy homes throughout the United States to use as grow houses.[93]

In fact, the number, location of, and compliance issues of California dispensaries continue to be serious issues, especially for the cities of Los Angeles and San Diego. In these cities, local police departments must field neighbors' complaints about dispensaries as well as enforce federal laws, such as where such dispensaries can be located and whom they can serve.

Some studies suggest the opposite, that dispensaries do not increase crime. For example, Bridget Freisthler, an associate professor of social welfare at UCLA's Luskin School of Public Affairs, found that dispensaries tended to be located in wealthy neighborhoods, such as Venice, Hollywood, and Westwood, that already had lower crime rates. In her 2007 study, Freisthler found that living within 100 feet of a marijuana dispensary was safer than living near a liquor store or restaurant, when crime statistics were compared.

However, Friesthler believes the issue requires further study. She suspects that dispensaries do not necessarily reduce crime. She thinks that areas such as South Los Angeles already have an established illegal market, and few legal dispensaries are located in these high crime areas. Thus crime may simply remain high in the same areas. Frieisthler received a $2.7 million grant from the National Institutes of Health to further study the relationship between crime and medical marijuana.

Driving Under the Influence

Another conundrum in the debate is determining how states should deal with people driving under the influence of medical marijuana. Attorney Sean McAllister describes the problem law enforcement officials are facing: "The explosion of medical marijuana patients has led to a lot of drivers sticking the (marijuana) card in law enforcement's face, saying, 'You can't do anything to me, I'm legal.'"[94]

Driving under the influence of any drug, however, is illegal in all 50 states, and a large body of research shows that marijuana has a measurable, although mild, effect on drivers' motor skills, causing slow reaction times and increasing the likelihood that drivers will drift and swerve. Proposed solutions include setting a legal limit for marijuana—measured by how much THC drivers can have in their blood—similar to the blood alcohol tests that are widely used to ascertain whether a driver is drunk.

A number of state legislatures, such as those of Colorado and Washington, are currently debating what these legal thresholds should be. For now, these proposals are fraught with controversy due to a lack of conclusive data on the level of THC that renders a driver impaired and whether marijuana intoxication plays a significant role in motor vehicle crashes. At the same time, others worry that putting an impaired-driving limit on marijuana could garner support for marijuana legalization in general.

Reevaluation Needed?

Clearly, the state legalization of medical marijuana has led to quandaries about how to enforce federal laws while protecting patients who may legally use the drug to treat illnesses. These quandaries have led a small but vocal minority to suggest that mari-

Prospective customers check out different varieties of marijuana available from an Oakland medical marijuana dispensary. Public sentiment is mixed on the effect such dispensaries have on neighborhood crime.

juana should be legalized federally so that its use can be regulated and enforced consistently throughout the country. This minority cites the fact that medical communities have found nothing harmful in marijuana use. Years of study have influenced doctors to see the clear benefits of the drug and have also increased confidence that its negative ramifications remain small. For example, the American College of Physicians (ACP) strongly believes that physicians who prescribe or dispense medical marijuana in accordance with state law should be exempt from federal criminal prosecution, civil liability, or professional sanctioning, such as loss of licensure or credentialing. Similarly, ACP strongly urges protection from criminal or civil penalties for patients who "use medical marijuana as permitted under state laws."[95]

In 2009 the prestigious American Medical Association urged a reclassification of Schedule I status and called for more research:

> Our AMA urges that marijuana's status as a federal Schedule I controlled substance be reviewed with the goal of facilitating the conduct of clinical research and development of cannabinoid-based medicines, and alternate delivery methods. This should not be viewed as an endorsement of state-based medical cannabis programs, the legalization of marijuana, or that scientific evidence on the therapeutic use of cannabis meets the current standards for a prescription drug product.[96]

"[The American Medical Association] urges that marijuana's status as a federal Schedule I controlled substance be reviewed with the goal of facilitating the conduct of clinical research and development of cannabinoid-based medicines."[96]

— American Medical Association.

Fewer Raids?

The federal government also seems to be tiring of its stance on prosecuting marijuana users. In 2009 the US attorney general, Eric Holder, announced that DEA raids would end on state-approved marijuana dispensaries. The new policy represents a significant turnaround for the federal government.

The US Department of Justice also amended its position in 2009. It issued a memo, known as the Ogden memo, after deputy attorney general David Ogden, to clarify its position on the medical use of marijuana and provide parameters to federal prosecutors in states where medical marijuana is legal. The memo states, in part, that prosecutors should not target "individuals whose actions are in clear and unambiguous compliance with existing state laws providing for the medical use of marijuana."[97] Specifically, individuals with cancer or other serious illnesses who use medical marijuana and the caregivers who provide the medical marijuana in accordance with state law should not be the focus of federal prosecution.

Yet this softening is again contradicted by other statements that allow for prosecution of anyone found in noncompliance with federal laws. The memo also states clearly that "prosecution of commercial enterprises that unlawfully market and sell marijuana for profit continues to be an enforcement priority."[98]

The DEA makes it clear that it is safeguarding against any increase in recreational use and that it also believes the evidence points to medical marijuana laws leading to more recreational use: "The popularity of these THC-like synthetic cannabinoids has significantly increased throughout the United States, and they are being abused for their psychoactive properties as reported by law enforcement, the medical community, and through scientific literature."[99] For now, at least, the United States must sometimes walk an uncomfortably narrow rail between state and federal law. Studies in the states where medical marijuana is legal will continue to investigate the effects medical marijuana has on the community.

"The popularity of these THC-like synthetic cannabinoids has significantly increased throughout the United States, and they are being abused for their psychoactive properties."[99]

— Drug Enforcement Administration.

Facts

- According to the California Police Chiefs Association, fires caused by unsafe indoor marijuana growing operations are becoming increasingly common, posing a risk to surrounding residential areas.

- A 2011 Rand Corporation study concluded that crime actually escalates when legal marijuana dispensaries are shut down, but Rand withdrew the study after the federal government protested its findings.

- According to the Federal Bureau of Investigation, over 800,000 people are prosecuted each year for marijuana violations.

- The 2010 *Monitoring the Future* report states that 1 in 15 students in tenth and twelfth grades uses pot on a daily or near daily basis.

- Assessing data from the National Highway Traffic Safety Administration over a 10-year period, researchers found that fatal car crashes decreased by 9 percent in states that legalized marijuana use.

Source Notes

Introduction: A Human Story

1. James Francis, "Terminal Cancer," RxMarijuana.com, March 9, 2012. http://rxmarijuana.com.
2. Francis, "Terminal Cancer."
3. John Koch, "The Impact of Medical Marijuana in Oregon," Oregon State Sheriff's Association, Spring 2010. www.oregonsheriffs.org.

Chapter One: What Are the Origins of the Medical Marijuana Debate?

4. Ethan Russo et al., "Phytochemical and Genetic Analyses of Ancient Cannabis from Central Asia," *Journal of Experimental Botany*, November 2008. http://jxb.oxfordjournals.org.
5. Quoted in Larry Sloman, *Reefer Madness: The History of Marijuana in America*. New York: St. Martin's Griffin, 1979, p. 22.
6. Quoted in Sloman, *Reefer Madness*, p. 30.
7. Quoted in Sloman, *Reefer Madness*, p. 63.
8. William Woodward, statement, *Marijuana Tax Act of 1937: Hearing on H.R. 6906 Before the US Congress, Senate Committee on Finance, Taxation of Marihuana*, July 10, 1937.
9. Quoted in Lester Grinspoon, "History of Cannabis as a Medicine," Multidisciplinary Association for Psychedelic Studies, August 16, 2005. www.maps.org.
10. Quoted in Stuff Stoners Like, "Medical Marijuana Is the Result of the Relationship Between Two Gay Men," March 31, 2010. http://stuffstonerslike.com.
11. Quoted in Grinspoon, "History of Cannabis as Medicine."
12. National Commission on Marihuana and Drug Abuse, *Marihuana: A Signal of Misunderstanding*, March 1972. www.druglibary.org.
13. Institute of Medicine, *Marijuana and Medicine: Assessing the Science Base*. Washington, DC: National Academies Press, 1999, p. 179.
14. Institute of Medicine, *Marijuana and Medicine*, p. 179.
15. Institute of Medicine, *Marijuana and Medicine*, p. 179.

16. Barry McCaffrey, letter to Donna Shalala, April 20, 1999. http://medicalmarijuanaprocon.org.

17. Quoted in Marijuana Policy Project, "Medical Marijuana Overview," December 12, 2011. www.mpp.org.

Chapter Two: Is Marijuana Effective Medicine?

18. Anna Wilde Mathews, "Is Marijuana a Medicine?" *Wall Street Journal*, January 18, 2010. www.wallstreetjournal.com.

19. Quoted in *Economist*, "Reefer Madness," April 27, 2006. www.economist.com.

20. Daniel I. Abrams et al., "Cannabis in Painful HIV-Associated Sensory Neuropathy: A Randomized Placebo-Controlled Trial," *Neurology*, February 13, 2007. www.neurology.org.

21. Quoted in John Ingold, "Medical-Marijuana Advocates Seek Society's Approval," *Denver Post*, July 4, 2010. www.denverpost.com.

22. Quoted in Randy Dotinga, "The Gaps in Medical Marijuana Knowledge," Voice of San Diego, November 18, 2011. www.voiceofsandiego.org.

23. Quoted in ScienceDaily, "Smoked Medical Cannabis May Be Beneficial as Treatment for Chronic Neuropathic Pain, Study Suggests," August 30, 2010. www.sciencedaily.com.

24. Quoted in Megan Burke and Maureen Cavanaugh, "Health Effects of Marijuana," KPBS, September 27, 2010. www.kpbs.org.

25. Quoted in Ingold, "Medical-Marijuana Advocates Seek Society's Approval."

26. Quoted in Brian Newsome, "Scientists, FDA at Odds over Benefits of Marijuana," *Gazette*, May 2, 2009. www.gazette.com.

27. Quoted in Newsome, "Scientists, FDA at Odds over Benefits of Marijuana."

28. Institute of Medicine, *Marijuana and Medicine*, p. 179.

29. Quoted in Courtney Hutchinson, "Marijuana Advocates Sue Feds After DEA Rejects Weed as Medicine," Americans for Safe Access, July 12, 2011. http://safeaccessnow.org.

30. Quoted in Brian Montopoli, "Does the Pot Pill Work?," CBS News, November 9, 2009. www.cbsnews.com.

31. Quoted in Montopoli, "Does the Pot Pill Work?"

32. Quoted in Ed Rosenthal and Steve Kubby, *Why Marijuana Should Be Legal*. New York: Thunder's Mouth, 1996, p. 74.

33. Richard Saslow, letter to the editor, *New York Times*, December 14, 2011. www.nytimes.com.

34. Center for Medicinal Cannabis Research, *Report to the Legislature and Governor of the State of California Presenting Findings Pursuant to SB847 Which Created the CMCR and Provided State Funding*, February 11, 2010. www.cmcr.ucsd.edu.

35. Quoted in *PBS NewsHour*, "Doctors, Patients Assess Effectiveness of Medical Marijuana," August 23, 2011. www.pbs.org.

36. Patrick Fox, "The Effect of Cannabis on Tremor in Patients with Multiple Sclerosis," *Neurology*, April 2004. www.neurology.org.

37. Quoted in Montopoli, "Does the Pot Pill Work?"

38. Quoted in *PBS NewsHour*, "Doctors, Patients Assess Effectiveness of Medical Marijuana."

39. Quoted in *PBS Newshour*, "Doctors, Patients Assess Effectiveness of Medical Marijuana."

40. National Eye Institute, "Glaucoma and Marijuana Use," March 17, 2009. http://nei.nih.gov.

41. American Medical Association, "Use of Cannabis for Medicinal Purposes," Council of Science and Public Health. www.ama-assn.org.

42. American Medical Association, "Use of Cannabis for Medicinal Purposes."

43. Quoted in Drug Enforcement Administration, "The DEA Position on Marijuana," January 2011. www.justice.gov.

Chapter Three: What Are the Risks of Medical Marijuana?

44. R. Gil Kerlikowske, "Why Marijuana Legalization Would Compromise Public Health and Public Safety," speech, California Police Chiefs Association Conference, March 4, 2010. www.whitehouse.gov.

45. Quoted in Sarah Kershaw and Rebecca Cathcart, "Marijuana Is Gateway Drug for Two Debates," *New York Times*, July 17, 2009. www.nytimes.com.

46. Quoted in Brian Montopoli, "Does the Pot Pill Work?"

47. Quoted in Kershaw and Cathcart, "Marijuana Is Gateway Drug for Two Debates."

48. Quoted in Burke and Cavanaugh, "Health Effects of Marijuana."

49. British Lung Foundation, "A Smoking Gun? The Impact of Cannabis Smoking on Respiratory Health," November 11, 2002. www.ukcia.org.

50. Quoted in Russ Belville, "Sanjay Gupta: What the Next Surgeon General Doesn't Know About Pot," AlterNet, January 8, 2009. www.alternet.org.

51. Robert Melamide, "Cannabis and Tobacco Smoke Are Not Equally Carcinogenic," *Harm Reduction Journal*, 2005. www.harmreduction-journal.com.

52. Mark Pletcher, "Association Between Marijuana Exposure and Pulmonary Function over 20 Years," *Journal of the American Medical Association*, January 11, 2012. http://jama.ama-assn.org.

53. National Highway Traffic Safety Administration, "Drugs and Human Performance Fact Sheets," April 2004. www.nhtsa.gov.

54. Kerlikowske, "Why Marijuana Legalization Would Compromise Public Health and Public Safety."

55. Kimia Honarmand, Mary C. Tierney, Paul O'Connor, and Anthony Feinstein, "Effects of Cannabis on Cognitive Function in Patients with Multiple Sclerosis," *Neurology*, March 2011. www.neurology.org.

56. Quoted in Mikaela Conley, "Early and Chronic Marijuana Use May Damage Brain Function, Says Study," ABC News, November 15, 2010. http://abcnews.go.com.

57. Quoted in Conley, "Early and Chronic Marijuana Use May Damage Brain Function, Says Study."

58. Quoted in Maia Szalavitz, "Study: Marijuana Not Linked with Long-Term Cognitive Impairment," *Time*, July 19, 2011. http://healthland.time.com.

59. Patrik Roser, "No Association Between Chronic Cannabis Use and Loudness Dependence of Auditory Evoked Potentials as Indicator of Central Serotonergic Neurotransmission," *Neuroscience Letters*, September 2009. www.journals.elsevier.

60. Anonymous, comment, "The Link Between Marijuana Use and Panic and Anxiety," HealthyPlace.com. www.healthyplace.com.

61. Quoted in Sarah Baldauf, "Teen Depression Worsened by Marijuana, Government Says," *US News & World Report*, May 9, 2008. www.usnews.com.

62. D.H. Linszen, "Cannabis Use and Age at Onset of Symptoms in Subjects at Clinical High Risk for Psychosis," *Acta Psychiatrica Scandinavica*, July 12, 2011. www.blackwellpublishing.com.

63. Joseph M. Pierre, "Cannabis, Synthetic Cannabinoids, and Psychosis Risk: What the Evidence Says," *Current Psychiatry*, September 2011. www.currentpsychiatry.com.

Chapter Four: Can Medical Marijuana Improve Health?

64. Cannabis Healing, "Psychological Conditions." www.cannabishealing.com.

65. Quoted in Krystal Harwell, "Medical Marijuana—Why It Shouldn't Be Illegal," Gather, September 25, 2007. www.gather.com.

66. Quoted in Voice of San Diego, "The Gaps in Medical Marijuana Knowledge," November 18, 2011. www.voiceofsandiego.org.

67. Frank Lucido, "Implementation of the Compassionate Use Act in a Family Medical Practice: Seven Years Clinical Experience," DrFrankLucido.com. http://drfranklucido.com.

68. Kurt Blaas, "Treating Depression with Cannabinoids," *Cannabinoids*, 2008. www.cannabis-med.org.

69. Blaas, "Treating Depression with Cannabinoids."

70. Office of National Drug Control Policy/Executive Office of the President, "Teen Marijuana Use Worsens Depression: An Analysis of Recent Data Shows 'Self-Medicating' Could Actually Make Things Worse," May 2008. www.theantidrug.com.

71. Quoted in Drug Enforcement Administration, "The DEA Position on Marijuana," January 2011. www.justice.gov.

72. Quoted in ScienceDaily, "Cannabis: Potent Anti-depressant in Low Doses, Worsens Depression at High Doses," October 23, 2007. www.sciencedaily.com.

73. Patsy K. Eagan, "Pot Stirring," *Elle*, July 18, 2008. www.elle.com.

74. Quoted in Mickey Martin, *Medical Marijuana 101.* Oakland, CA: Quick American, 2011, pp. 34–35.

75. Quoted in Lester Grinspoon and James Bakalar, "The Use of Cannabis as a Mood Stabilizer in Bipolar Disorder: Anecdotal Evidence and the Need for Clinical Research," *Journal of Psychoactive Drugs*, April/June 1998. http://rxmarijuana.com.

76. Jay Cavanaugh, "Cannabis and Depression," American Alliance for Medical Cannabis. www.letfreedomgrow.com.

77. Quoted in *Insight Journal*, "Marijuana Use Linked to Bipolar Disorder—Which Came First?," 2007. www.anxiety-and-depression -solutions.com.

78. Quoted in Office of National Drug Control Policy/Executive Office of the President, "The Link Between Marijuana & Mental Illness," July 2007. www.theantidrug.com.

79. Quoted in Jeff Brady, "Can Marijuana Ease PTSD? A Debate Brews," NPR, May 19, 2010. www.npr.org.

80. Quoted in Brady, "Can Marijuana Ease PTSD? A Debate Brews."

81. Quoted in Maia Szalavitz, "More Evidence That Marijuana-like Drugs May Help Prevent PTSD," *Time*, September 23, 2011. www.time.com.

82. Quoted in Brady, "Can Marijuana Ease PTSD? A Debate Brews."

83. Quoted in Cannabis Healing, "Medical Marijuana in California, 1996–2006." www.cannabishealing.com.

84. Seth Ammerman, "Medical Marijuana: Update for the Pediatrician," *California Pediatrician*, Winter 2011, pp. 12–13.

85. Quoted in ScienceDaily, "UC Irvine Researchers Demonstrate How Marijuana-Like Chemicals Work in the Brain," March 23, 1999. www.sciencedaily.com.

Chapter Five: How Should the Medical Use of Marijuana Be Regulated?

86. Quoted in John Hoeffel, "US Decrees That Marijuana Has No Accepted Medical Use," *Los Angeles Times*, July 9, 2011. http://articles.latimes.com.

87. Quoted in *PBS NewsHour*, "California Raids Threaten Medical Marijuana Regulation," November 8, 2011. www.pbs.org.

88. Quoted in *PBS NewsHour*, "California Raids Threaten Medical Marijuana Regulation."

89. Quoted in Burke and Cavanaugh, "Health Effects of Marijuana."

90. Quoted in Maia Szalavitz, "Study: Legal Medical Marijuana Doesn't Encourage Kids to Smoke More Pot," *Time*, November 3, 2011. http://healthland.time.com.

91. Quoted in Szalavitz, "Study: Legal Medical Marijuana Doesn't Encourage Kids to Smoke More Pot."

92. Karen O'Keefe and Mitch Earleywine, "Marijuana Use by Young People: The Impact of State Marijuana Laws," Marijuana Policy Project, June 2011. www.mpp.org.

93. California Police Chiefs Association's Task Force on Marijuana Dispensaries, "White Paper on Marijuana Dispensaries," 2009, p. 10.

94. Quoted in Kristen Wyatt, "Stoned Driving Epidemic Puts Wrinkle in Pot Debate," *San Diego Union-Tribune*, March 18, 2012. www.utsandiego.com.

95. American College of Physicians, "Supporting Research into the Therapeutic Role of Marijuana," February 15, 2008. http://acponline.org.

96. American Medical Association, "Use of Cannabis for Medicinal Purposes," November 10, 2009. www.ama-assn.org.

97. US Department of Justice, "Memorandum for Selected United States Attorneys," October 19, 2009. www.justice.gov.

98. US Department of Justice, "Memorandum for Selected United States Attorneys."

99. Drug Enforcement Administration, "Schedules of Controlled Substances: Temporary Placement of Five Synthetic Cannabinoids into Schedule I," March 1, 2011. http://dea.gov.

Related Organizations and Websites

American Alliance for Medical Cannabis (AAMC)
44500 Tide Ave.
Arch Cape, OR 97102
phone: (503) 436-1882
e-mail: contact@letfreedomgrow.com
website: www.letfreedomgrow.com

AAMC is an advocacy group that is dedicated to promoting the rights of medical marijuana patients. It provides information on common medical uses and benefits of marijuana.

Americans for Safe Access (ASA)
1322 Webster St., Suite 402
Oakland, CA 94612
phone: (510) 251-1856
e-mail: infor@safeaccessnow.org
website: www.safeaccessnow.org

ASA is an organization of patients, doctors, scientists, and others concerned with ensuring access to marijuana for medical use and research. ASA promotes legislation, education, and grassroots actions that support safe and legal access for patients and their caregivers.

Center for Medicinal Cannabis Research (CMCR)

220 Dickinson St., Suite B
San Diego, CA 92103
phone: (619) 543-5024
e-mail: cmcr@ucsd.edu
website: www.cmcr.ucsd.edu

Established at the University of California at San Diego, CMCR conducts research, including human studies, on the safety and efficacy of medical marijuana. The center's published research is described on its website, along with additional educational resources.

Drug Free America Foundation, Inc. (DFAF)

5999 Central Ave., Suite 301
Saint Petersburg, FL 33710
phone: (727) 828-0211
website: www.dfaf.org

DFAF is a drug prevention organization that develops and promotes policies and legislation to reduce illegal drug use and the problems associated with it. The foundation opposes the decriminalization or legalization of marijuana for medical use.

Drug Policy Alliance (DPA)

70 W. Thirty-Sixth St., 16th Floor
New York, NY 10018
phone: (212) 613-8020
e-mail: nyc@drugpolicy.org
website: www.drugpolicy.org

DPA supports state initiatives that would render marijuana legal and accessible to patients and their caregivers. The alliance publishes position papers, research briefs, and fact sheets.

Drug Watch International

PO Box 45218
Omaha, NE 68145
phone: (402) 384-9212
website: www.drugwatch.org

Drug Watch International is a nonprofit organization that opposes the legalization of all illicit drugs. The group supports drug education and prevention programs as well as law enforcement strategies aimed at reducing drug use and trafficking.

Marijuana Policy Project (MMP)

236 Massachusetts Ave. NE, Suite 400
Washington, DC 20002
phone: (202) 462-5747
e-mail: info@mpp.org
website: www.mpp.org

MMP advocates the responsible use of marijuana for medical and nonmedical purposes. The group works to increase public awareness about marijuana and to reform laws that prohibit its use.

National Center on Addiction and Substance Abuse (CASA)

Columbia University
633 Third Ave., 19th Floor
New York, NY 10017
phone: (212) 841-5200
website: www.casacolumbia.org

CASA is a science-based organization that seeks to educate the public about the dangers of drug abuse and addiction. The center publishes a variety of research-based papers on those topics.

National Institute on Drug Abuse (NIDA)

National Institutes of Health
6001 Executive Blvd., Room 5213
Bethesda, MD 20892
phone: (301) 443-1124
e-mail: information@nida.nih.gov
website: www.nida.niha.gov

NIDA is a division of the National Institutes of Health, which is part of the US Department of Health and Human Services. NIDA sponsors and conducts research on drug abuse and addiction. It publishes a variety of educational materials on marijuana.

National Organization for the Reform of Marijuana Laws (NORML)

1600 K St. NW, Suite 501
Washington, DC 20006
phone: (202) 483-5500
e-mail: norml@norml.org
website: www.norml.org

NORML works to increase public support for the end of marijuana prohibition for both medical and recreational use. The organization lobbies for marijuana policy reform and publishes educational materials on its website.

Office of National Drug Control Policy (ONDCP)

Drug Policy Information Clearinghouse
PO Box 6000
Rockville, MD 20849
phone: (800) 666-3332
e-mail: http://ondcp@ncjrs.org
website: www.whitehousedrugpolicy.gov

ONDCP oversees the nation's drug control program and publishes many educational materials, including information on marijuana.

Wo/Men's Alliance for Medical Marijuana (WAMM)

309 Cedar St., #39
Santa Cruz, CA 95060
phone: (831) 425-0580
e-mail: info@wamm.org
website: www.wamm.org

WAMM is made up of patients who seek safe and legal access to medical marijuana as treatment for terminal or debilitating illnesses.

Additional Reading

Books

Greg Campbell, *Pot, Inc.: Inside Medical Marijuana, America's Most Outlaw Industry*. New York: Sterling, 2012.

Steve Fox, Paul Armentano, and Mason Vert, *Marijuana Is Safer: So Why Are We Driving People to Drink?* White River Junction, VT: Chelsea Green, 2009.

John Geluardi, *Cannabiz: The Explosive Rise of the Medical Marijuana Industry*. Sausalito, CA: Polipoint, 2010.

Albert T. Johnson, *Medical Marijuana and Marijuana Use*. New York: Nova Science, 2009.

Mark A.R. Kleiman, Jonathan Caulkins, and Angela Hawken, *Drugs and Drug Policy: What Everyone Needs to Know*. New York: Oxford University Press, 2011.

Michael Kuhar, *The Addicted Brain: Why We Abuse Drugs, Alcohol, and Nicotine*. Upper Saddle River, NJ: FT Press, 2011.

Martin Lee, *Smoke Signals: A Social History of Marijuana—Medical, Recreational, and Scientific*. New York: Scribner, 2012.

Mickey Martin, *Medical Marijuana 101*. Oakland, CA: Quick American, 2011.

Trish Regan, *Joint Ventures: Inside America's Almost Legal Marijuana Industry*. Hoboken, NJ: Wiley, 2011.

Robin Room, Benedict Fischer, Wayne Hall, Simon Lenton, and Peter Reuter, *Cannabis Policy: Moving Beyond Stalemate*. New York: Oxford University Press, 2010.

Periodicals

Hal Arkowitz and Scott O. Lilienfeld, "Experts Tell the Truth About Pot," *Scientific American*, February 22, 2012.

Jessica Bennett, "Down, but Not Burnt Out," Daily Beast, November 3, 2010. www.thedailybeast.com.

Brian Doherty, "L.A.'s Pot Revolution," *Reason*, May 2010.

Kevin Drum, "Can California Legalize Marijuana?," *Mother Jones*, July 18, 2010.

Jan Gumbiner, "Does Marijuana Cause Cancer?," *Psychology Today*, February 17, 2011.

John Hoeffel, "US Decrees That Marijuana Has No Accepted Medical Use, *Los Angeles Times*, July 9, 2011.

Kirk Johnson, "Marijuana Push in Colorado Likens It to Alcohol," *New York Times*, January 12, 2012.

Marie Myung-ok Lee, "My Mother-in-Law's One High Day," *New York Times*, December 9, 2011.

Dinah Miller and Annette Hanson, "Medical Marijuana Laws Make a Farce of Medicine," *Baltimore Sun*, March 7, 2012.

Lucy Steigerwald, "Study: Medical Marijuana Doesn't Make the Kids More Reefer-Mad in Rhode Island," *Reason*, November 3, 2011.

John Suthers, "Commentary: Medical Marijuana a Threat to State's Children," *Education News*, February 6, 2012.

Maia Szalavitz, "Why Medical Marijuana Laws Reduce Traffic Deaths, *Time*, December 2, 2011.

Donald Tashkin, "Does Smoking Marijuana Increase the Risk of Chronic Obstructive Pulmonary Disease?," *Canadian Medical Association Journal*, April 14, 2009.

Daniel B. Wood, "Confusion Reigns over Medical Marijuana as States and Feds Clash," *Christian Science Monitor*, December 13, 2011.

Index